Answering America's Problem

Answering America's Problem

Alesia Graham

To order additional copies of this book, contact:
Xlibris Corporation
1-888-795-4274
www.Xlibris.com
Orders@Xlibris.com
45069

CONTENTS

To you and to the people of the world.

Another inspiring message from God to his people,

to reveal the trick the enemy is using to try to destroy the people of the world.

Jesus said, "The thief cometh not, but for to steal, and to kill, and to destroy: but I am come that they might have life, and that they might have it more abundantly." (St. John 10:10)

ACKNOWLEDGMENT

Every opportunity I get to acknowledge the Holy Spirit I must take advantage of, because truly the Holy Spirit has been faithful to me. I can recall when my writing career began. It happened one day when I was communing with the Spirit concerning the body of Christ that is the church. Since becoming born again and being baptized with the Holy Ghost, I have always communed with the Spirit. I have attended many church services and Bible study sessions, and on many occasions I have heard ministers teaching and speaking about the great works that Jesus did, how God and Jesus are one, and how they are the same yesterday, today, and forever. Therefore for many days I had been questioning the Holy Spirit concerning these sayings. If it was true, I wanted to know why the works that Jesus did yesterday are not happening today. So on this day when the Holy Spirit and I were talking he began to give to me the reason that the work that Jesus had done was not taking place today. I began writing what the Spirit was revealing. So much was being revealed that finally I asked the Spirit what was this he was giving me. I thought it was a message, but he told me that it was a book.

Being overcome with joy I had to stop writing for a while, so I decided to go to the store to get some tools that I would need if I was indeed going to write a book. I returned to writing the next day and continued writing off and on for the next seven days, until the Spirit finished speaking to me concerning the matter. When the manuscript was finished I called it "What Is Wrong with the Body of Christ." I was so excited about what had taken place, and I told the Spirit that I would use the proceeds from the book to fund the work of God—not realizing what I had said to God or understanding the impact that it had on him, until he began making known to me another revelation. This revelation concerned the answer to America's problem.

By now I realized that God had gifted me to write so I continued over a long period of time to write this second manuscript and when I had finished writing the Spirit said to me, "Now this one is yours." I tell you the floodgate of tears was opened and I just could not stop the tears from running. I began to think, who am I to God that I have been favored like this. So I hope you can now understand why I must always acknowledge the Holy Spirit—it is he who has made this book possible.

INTRODUCTION

A problem, according to Webster's Dictionary, is any question or matter involving doubt, uncertainty, or difficulty. Before a problem can be solved, it must first be determined that a problem exists. It has clearly been identified that America and the rest of the world have a serious problem. This problem has many faces—tragedies, 9/11, school shootings, bombing, kidnapping, child molestation, national disasters, gangs, and war just to name a few—but there are many others.

Without any doubt, America and the rest of the world have a problem. The question now is, What are we going to do about this problem and what method should we use? The first thing to know is that there is only one problem that America has, and that the world has—just one problem, although it has taken on many faces. This book is written to get to the root of the problem in America and the world, and to expose the seed that is the origin of the problem. Thereafter rendering a solution based upon the word of God. Biblical solutions can be used not only to identify and resolve problems in America, they can also be used to solve problems around the world. Any problem can be resolved though biblical methods once it has been established biblically what the problem is.

CHAPTER ONE

IDENTIFYING THE PROBLEM

If the solution to a problem is to be made known, it must first be determined where the problem originated. A comparable scenario would be visiting your primary physician; one of the first things that is requested is a family history. History is important because it is the branch of knowledge that deals with past events. It plays a key role in the healing and treatment process by providing a target of defense. It is also helpful in determining diagnosis.

This same approach can also be used in solving most problems as well as conditions. Knowing that a problem will never cease until the root has been totally destroyed is essential. This makes searching for the root the first priority, because within the root lies the lifeline, and as long as there is root, there is life whether it is good or bad. Therefore, the first step that should be taken when dealing with a problem or a condition is locating the root, which is not only the lifeline, but also serves as the foundation, the base, the support that enables stability and continuance.

Now when dealing with a situation that causes stress, heartache, and pain—such as terrorism—searching for the root means realizing the origin of the problem. We the people must take a moment to remember that the enemy is cunning and crafty and his intention is to steal, kill, and destroy. This thought must always remain in the forefront of every mind. The devil our enemy operates through methods of distraction and deception, he uses the power given to him by the target source.

He is powerless working alone, but the spirit of belief is powerful whether the thought is good or bad. Therefore, when the doctrine of the devil is believed and the word of God is not believed, evil is produced. This evil work can be observed where there is no knowledge of the word of God, or where there is disobedience to the word. Whatever the case may be it creates an atmosphere where the devil can operate. The devil's work is always the opposite of God, just as the opposite of cold is hot. God is good, and he desires goodness for his people. The devil is evil, and he desires bad things to happen to people. His number one goal is to try to prove to the people that God is not who he said he is, and he cannot or will not do what he said he would do. But all unrighteousness is the work of the devil. He is the enemy, and he is the terrorist, and his job is to terrorize. If we the people would remove all bad thoughts, we would put the terrorist to death; and if we would remove all unrighteous acts, we would like Jesus destroy the works of the devil.

As a prophet of God, I do not believe there had to be a physical war to win the war on terror. But I do believe that because we have allowed the word of God to have no effect through our disobedience, sin has caused us to lose hope, help, and the shelter of God. And therefore, wars and rumors are the enemy. The Bible teaches us that there will be wars and rumors of wars. These words were recorded over two thousand years ago. How was it made known that many years ago, what would be happening today in 2005-2006? It was made known because God the Father is omniscient; he knew that man would be disobedient during this time, and that he would bring calamity upon himself.

When God spoke about wars and rumors of wars, he was not talking about killing only, he was also speaking about disputes and disagreements. In Isaiah 1:18 when God said, Come let us reason together, he was revealing a solution to disagreements. When we the people do not understand the mind of God, many times we misinterpret his words. There is a physical side and a spiritual side to everything, and when we do not understand God who is the ruler of the spiritual world, we are forced to live according to the principles ruling the physical world.

In the physical world come all the troubles which we see and which we are experiencing today. We are spiritual beings living in physical bodies; therefore, our lifestyle should be patterned after the spiritual world living according to spiritual principles, which is the command of God. But this is not how we are living; we live according to man's ways and ideas, which are contrary to God's.

Whenever we do not keep the ways of God, we bring the curses that are written in the book of Deuteronomy chapter 28, into our lives. These curses speak to the physical man, and when they are activated, they are set in motion, and nothing can stop them except if man returns to the ways of God. These curses are lying dormant, and they must be endured once they are activated. Disobeying the commandments means they remain in operation until repentance or destruction takes place. Many people may not understand this concept, but I will explain it to you.

But before I do, I must tell you that God is not the reason bad things happen to people. People are the reason bad things happen to people. Let us think about ourselves as parents. Let us think about some of the things that we do when our children disobey us. This is a small-scale scenario of what is happening on earth between God and man. God created the devil to punish disobedience so that evil would not possess the land. God gave man dominion over the earth; therefore, man has the power to bring good or evil into creation by his ways and his deeds. The devil only has access to our lives when we disobey the word of God. So please understand that we are in control of our lives through the choices that we make. If we choose to obey God, the devil has no access to our life. If we choose not to obey God, the devil gets access to our life. This is why God commands us to do certain things. He is trying to protect us from the devil. It is the same thing we do when we are trying to protect our children, but just as they are hardheaded sometimes and refuse to obey, so likewise are we. If we choose to listen to God and do what he is commanding us to do, we can escape the evil that is abroad in the earth today.

When bad things happen to us, God is the most saddened because he loves his people more than we love ourselves. Can you imagine God creating people so the devil could do bad things to them? No, this is farthest from the truth, for God so loved the world that he sent his only begotten son Jesus to die to redeem it from the very curses that are written in Deuteronomy chapter 28. Because of Jesus, we do not have to die in sin; we can repent for our sins, and we can make mistakes. We can err and we can repent and try again and again. If God did not love us, he would not have created us, which was in his power to do or not to do. But we cause bad things to happen through disobedience. It does not have to be this way. If we would obey the commandments, we could live in the blessings of God. These blessings are recorded in Deuteronomy chapter 28, which says that all these blessings will come upon us. This lets me know that we have a choice to make, and the outcome of our life is based upon that choice.

I have recorded the blessings and the curses recorded in Deuteronomy chapter 28 in the last chapter of this book for your convenience. As you read through the curses for disobedience, I believe you will find areas where you have fallen short, as I have done. I am hoping that you will also do as I have done—repent for your sins and turn from disobeying God's word. I can tell you that it will not be a one-day experience, it will become an ongoing process. I was amazed at all the different areas I was falling short in. So amazed that I want you to know the operation of Satan is so evil that it must be revealed. Again, I must say that the devil is powerless working alone. He is a spirit, and he needs a body to work through the same as God. He operates by using the power of the mind through influence and persuasion, and his motives are evil. There is a cliché often spoken that the mind is the devil's workshop, and this is true. He appears to people using distraction and deception techniques to provoke influence and persuade people into believing him. This method is used for the sole purpose of capturing the mind to gain access and control of the body, which he needs to carry out his dirty work.

CHAPTER TWO

THE DEVIL'S WORKSHOP

The mind is powerful, *it is the womb where thoughts are birthed*. When a thought enters the mind and is received, conception takes place. Conception means that the mind has received the thought, and the thought is then passed on to the subconscious mind to be birthed out. The subconscious mind is not responsible for controlling thoughts that enter it. It is only responsible for birthing whatever thoughts it receives, whether they are good or bad. For this reason, it is important to control our thoughts on the conscious level. Thoughts are controlled by choice; therefore, whatever thoughts we allow our mind to receive—good or bad—this is what the subconscious mind will birth when the thought enters this place.

When a thought of destruction is planted into the mind of a person and enters the subconscious where it is birthed, it will enable the person to destroy or to be destroyed. How often have we heard it being said, "You must be born again"? But we receive this saying as some meaningless cliché, not realizing the importance thereof. Becoming born again is necessary because every human being that is born of a woman is born with a mind that is capable of birthing out evil thoughts. Unless we are born again, we do not have the power to control our thoughts in life, and we do not understand the knowledge or the depth of good and evil.

Psalm 51:5   Behold, I was shapen in iniquity; and in sin did my mother conceive me.

John 3:7   Marvel not that I said unto thee, Ye must be born again.

How can we know if a thought is good or bad, and by what method can this be determined? One thing for sure, we do know that the devil's report is always false because he is a tree of evil; therefore, he cannot produce anything that is good. The word of God is a sure way to prepare our mind against the devil, and it will teach us what is right and what is wrong. It is an amazing thing to me to see the world faced with so many problems and to know that it all began with a thought. I wonder what the world would be like if we would control our thoughts. For many years, the enemy has been able to use us like puppets on a string, for so long in fact that he has brought us to this place, time, and state in which we now live, simply by possessing our minds and using our bodies. He has used us to kill each other, mistreat each other, steal, lie, and cheat each other. There is no evil great or small that we do not do to each other.

Can someone tell me how is it that the devil was able to convince so many of us into believing things that are not true? I will give the reason myself. He was able to convince us because we lack the knowledge we need to make the right choice that is required to keep the devil from using us against each other. There is one thing that the devil knows: he knows what area we lack knowledge in. He knows this because when he presents us with an idea, we cannot make the right choice that will turn him away. Can you believe that the devil knows the word of God, which we do not know? He is able to make such fools of us because we lack knowledge. He sees us as being stupid, and he mocks us. Because of our stupidity, we do not know the difference between right and wrong. We have no knowledge of the word of God—the very thing that will teach us the tricks of the devil.

But I believe that with the help of the Almighty God, we will get to the root of terrorism, and we will win the war on terror, if this is what we want to do. We must remember that war starts on the thought level, not on the physical level, and therefore if we are going to disarm the enemy, we must be able to change the way people think. Becoming educated in the word and in the wisdom of God will equip us to do this.

Let me share with you something amazing that was made known to me by God: this revelation allowed me to know that conflicts and disputes can be won in debate and communication. But this type of victory will only come when people are skillful in the word and the wisdom of God. Let me begin sharing what God had revealed to me. If a dispute cannot be resolved during debate or communication, it usually becomes a physical conflict. As we know, when children begin to argue about something, if they are unable to settle the matter, arguing the dispute usually becomes a physical fight. This is the same tactic the devil uses in all his battles; he first creates disagreement between people. When there is no knowledge of the word of God or any wisdom of God present, the devil has control of the argument, and his thoughts are always evil.

Wisdom is being able to speak a word of reasoning that works for everyone involved. It does not matter who takes this step, long as someone involved in the dispute has the ability to speak a word of wisdom. If no one is able to speak a word of wisdom during a disagreement, there will be no grounds for reasoning, therefore closing the door to agreement and resolution. During these moments, conflicts can and usually do become physical. When the conflict reaches the physical level, the battle is no longer of the Lord; it is now controlled by Satan. And we know what he comes to do—steal, kill, and destroy. This is one of the reasons for the coming of the Lord Jesus Christ—so that we will no longer have to fight with sticks and stones.

The battle of the Lord is not a physical battle:

Ephesians 6: 12   For we wrestle not against flesh and blood, but against principalities, against powers, against the rulers of the darkness of this world, against spiritual wickedness in high places.

The lack of knowledge opens the door to physical war. We have been told of the power we possess in Jesus Christ, a power that will enable us to win every battle without lifting a finger. But when there is a lack of knowledge of the word of God, we have to fight with sticks and stones. This lack began back in creation when God gave man dominion over the earth. Man was given control over the earth. God gave it to him, and he is not going to come to the earth and do what he gave man the power to do. He told man if he would keep the commandments, good things would happen; and if he did not keep the commandments, bad things would happen. Therefore, man can control the whole earth by his ways and actions. But God knew bad things would happen upon the earth because he knew man would not do good deeds. Because man has an enemy who lives on earth with him, whose name is Lucifer; he is a spirit and he is the devil.

Man's first encounter with this spirit was in the Garden of Eden when God told Adam and Eve not to eat of the tree of knowledge of good and evil. God knew they would die spiritually if they ate of the fruit because God knows all things. Man does not know everything; this is why it is so important for man to obey God. But for some reason, man seems to have a hard time obeying God. The problem originated in the mind of man. If he could just learn to obey, he could save himself from a lot of trouble. Everything that has happened and everything that is going to happen has already been sent by God and recorded in his word. If man would educate himself in the word of God, it would teach him what to do to avoid certain troubles and calamities. It would teach him how to be aware of his enemies.

One major distraction—a dispute—put into action by the devil and that is taking place today is the focus of the attention of the people on the president as being America's problem. It may be a truth that the president is the agent of the devil used to carry out the attacks on America. It may even be said that he is the vessel the enemy has used to set in motion his destructive plan. But one thing for sure: the president is not the problem. Can you see how the enemy works against man? Do you really think that the president would intentionally put at risk the lives of the people? Degrading the president is not my assignment, my goal is to expose this hidden enemy working behind the scenes. America must understand her enemy and know that this is one of Satan's tricks to keep the country divided because the devil knows a divided house cannot stand.

We the people must remember that everything begins with a thought that is birthed into creation by the subconscious mind. A word of wisdom spoken in season has the power to cease any conflict by providing grounds for agreement and resolution. An amazing thing is to see and to know how many people think that there is no need for the Bible. But wisdom comes from God and knowledge of his word. If there is no knowledge of the word of God, how can wisdom come? These untrue statements spoken about the Bible today are just another trick of the devil because he knows that if he can cause the belief in the Bible to cease, he can rule the world.

All these things are taking place in the mind—it is the devil's workshop. The enemy knows that there is only one thing that can defeat him—that is the word of God; therefore, man must learn this. But how can man know the difference between right and wrong if there are no guidelines or bylaws? Guidelines are set in place by the owner, and the owner of the world is God. Every organization in existence today has bylaws—things that they will allow and things that they will not allow. If we, being earthly creatures, possess enough knowledge to set bylaws in place to keep order, how much more knowledgeable is our God who is the creator of all things? If God was mindful enough to give man a mind to establish laws to keep order in the things he rules over, don't you think that God had enough sense to establish laws to keep order on the earth over which he rules?

If the Bible, which contains the law and order of God, is removed, we are going to see destruction on earth the like of which we have never seen before. The tsunamis are nothing compared to what can happen if the word of God, which holds all things together, is removed. We are experiencing calamity all over the world today because of the lack of knowledge of God's word. The Bible is the bylaws of God. It is the order in which mankind should live; it is the very thing that is going to protect us against the enemy. If a man breaks the laws of the land, he is punished for doing so. Likewise, if we break the laws of God, we are punished. This punishment comes because we move ourselves from under the umbrella of protection and become exposed to the enemy, which happens through disobedience. The world is created to operate upon the laws of God automatically. The law was here before we were born. This is God's plan to keep evil from overtaking the world. If there were no words of God, we would have been consumed completely by now. There would be no living human upon the earth; the devil would have destroyed everyone. It is the word of God and those who have faith that is holding this world together today. Thank God for the believers. The loving father commands his people to obey him because he knows that if they disobey him, they will enter into automatic destruction. Once they have activated a curse because of disobedience, there is nothing God can do to help them until after they repent, obey the word, and turn away from that curse. How many curses will it take? How many lives will have to be lost before we turn back to God and repent? I hope by now you can see how important the word of God is, and how our mind is playing tricks on us.

CHAPTER THREE

THE LAW

If the bylaws governing an institution are removed, there will no longer be order, and this means anything goes. The bylaws are the very thing that provides a shelter and protection. The days of total destruction are fast approaching America because we live in a time where men and women have no desire to do what is right. Jesus spoke about these days.

Matthew 24:15-22   When you therefore shall see the abomination of desolation, spoken of by Daniel the prophet, stand in the holy place (whoso readeth, let him understand:)

Then let them which be in Judaea flee into the mountain:

Let him, which is on the housetop not come down to take any thing out of his house:

Neither let him, which is in the field return back to take his clothes.

And woe unto them that are with child, and to them that give suck in those days!

But pray ye that your flight be not in the winter, neither on the Sabbath day:

For then shall be great tribulation, such as was not since the beginning of the world to this time, no, nor ever shall be.

And except those days be shortened, there should no flesh be saved: but for the elect's sake those days shall be shortened.

The time has come for every American whose heart desires righteousness to take a stand. There are many that desire to operate in unrighteousness, and this is all right because God has given every one of us free will. Therefore we can choose to do what we want to do with our life as long as what we are doing does not affect others. Gays and lesbians have the right to get married if they want to, and women have the right to get an abortion if they want to. But the thing that God requires of us is that we know the consequences of the actions we take, and for those who know right from wrong to have nothing to do with evil. For the wages of sin is death, and the gift of God is eternal life.

Romans 6:23   For the wages of sin is death; but the gift of God is eternal life through Jesus Christ our lord.

Ministers are called to teach the word of God to the people. They are responsible for letting the people know what will happen when they make choices that are outside the will of God. The people need to know what effects our choices will have upon our lives and the society as a whole. God has given man free will, and yes, we do have a right to make decisions that are against the commands of God, but all the people need to know the outcome of the choice they make.

Proverbs 14:12   There is a way which seemeth right unto a man, but the end thereof are the ways of death.

If every woman having an abortion understood that she is breaking the law of God by committing murder and this is sin punishable by death, women would become afraid to get an abortion for fear they might die on the table. There is no fear of God upon the land today; this is why people are able to do the things they do. Even the word of God is not being preached with the fear of God; people are transgressing the laws of God as if he did not exist. But this one thing I can say, if we do not return to obeying the word of God, we have not seen anything yet. We do not want the angels to unleash judgment upon the land. What we are experiencing now are the plagues that are supposed to turn the people back to God. After the plagues comes judgment. God is holding back angels, allowing these disobedient behaviors to continue because he is giving us space to repent and turn away from sin. It is now time for the ministers of God to preach the truth of the word, if we are going to save the world. If the people continue to die in their sins, the blood will be acquired at the hands of the ministers. I believe this because God is going to hold someone accountable for the death of unborn, innocent children.

There are some choices that we can make that will cause death not only to ourselves, but also the curse will go down to the third and fourth generation, and people need to know this. People like to exempt themselves from being at fault by saying that such and such an offense was an error or a mistake. It may be true that some offenses are errors and some are mistakes, but we must remember that thoughts that are mistakes or errors come from the devil, and no one is exempt from having bad thoughts. The people need to be taught what to do when they have bad thoughts and bad ideas.

God does not give us thoughts that become mistakes or errors, because there is no mistake in God, and there is no error in him. It is important that we the people know what choice to make when these thoughts and ideas come. This knowledge and wisdom will be obtained as we read and study the word of God. It is understood that we will make wrong choices sometimes because we are not perfect and simply because we do not know everything. But we do need to be perfect in the things we do know, by doing what we know is right. When it becomes known to us that we have made a wrong decision, we need to correct the mistake immediately. Problems arrive when we do not correct the wrong choice. If we allow the error to continue, it is going to produce a bad result.

When we do not admit our faults, this is called deception, and deception is a work of the devil. This is the same tactic the devil used in the Garden of Eden when he deceived Adam and Eve. After the deception, the first thing Adam and Eve did was they hid themselves. This lesson teaches us that the spirit of deception will always cause you to cover up or to hide the matter. But we must learn that there is no winner when the spirit of deception is at work. The devil works as an undercover agent. He does not want what he is doing to be exposed, for fear that his plan may be stopped; therefore, he covers the matter until its outcome takes place. We can see this spirit at work in our young teenage girls who become pregnant. These young women hide the pregnancy, and when the time of delivery comes, they take a way out that usually causes death to the child and puts them in jail for murder. This is an example that proves that there are no winners when the devil is at work.

Can you imagine the damage the devil can do in a government? America will never be victorious over the war on terror if we continue to focus our attention on the leaders as being the problem. The devil is at work, and his work is evil. Does this exempt a participant involved in crime? No, because the devil is a spirit, and he needs a body to work through. If you yield your vessel to the devil, you must accept the consequences of your action. There are laws of the land in place to hold participants of evil accountable. But we must understand that during these times, the future of the country and the world and the well-being of the people are more important than the participants involved. There is a time for all things; the safety of the country and the well-being of the people are first priority. But this priority does not mean that we should omit dealing with the terror participants. We must understand that the problem with terror is much deeper than we think, and we must know that the enemy is the terrorist, and he has set terror in motion. The people involved in terrorism are nothing more than agents, and the saddest thing about all this is that terrorism is bigger than the player of the game is.

The devil is deceiving everyone because he does not have friends. He operates in such a way as to destroy all involved in his plan, even the players in the game. There are no winners in Satan's game except himself. The terrorist kills people, and people kill the terrorist; do you see any winners in this game? No one is winning but the devil, and he is after the soul of all human beings. The only way the soul of man can be received by God or the devil is for man to die first. God wants man to live because as long as there is life, there is hope that man will give his life to Christ, and his soul will return to God after his death. The devil wants man to die as soon as possible because if man dies outside of Christ, the devil gets the soul. This is the devil's reason for causing so much death. He is hoping that someone will perish before they have a chance to give their life to Christ.

CHAPTER FOUR

THE ORDER

Things do not just happen. When something happens or takes place, it is the reaction to an action. Everything is produced from a seed, which is the origin or the beginning. For example, fruits such as apples, oranges, and peaches do not just happen to appear, they come from fruit trees. The same with human beings and animals: they do not drop from the sky, they come by way of conception.

Likewise, good deeds or evil deeds do not just appear, they come by way of thoughts. Thoughts are the seeds that produce deeds, and they do not just pop into the mind, they come from a source. Everything has an origin, and when something is able to reproduce itself, it is a tree of origin. If God possesses the thoughts of a man, that man becomes a tree of righteousness. If the devil possesses the thoughts of a man that man becomes a tree of evil. People who are capable of evil are called devil. God's ways are not our ways, and his thoughts are not our thoughts. For this reason, seeking the mind of Christ is most important if we have any intention of mastering planet Earth.

Isaiah 55:8-9   For my thoughts are not your thoughts, neither are your ways my ways, saith the Lord.

For as the heavens are higher than the earth, so are my ways higher than your ways, and my thoughts than your thoughts.

Philippians 2:5   Let this mind be in you, which was also in Christ Jesus.

In the Garden of Eden, when God commanded Adam and Eve not to eat of the tree of knowledge of good and evil, God knew man did not know anything about evil because God had created him without that knowledge. Unto this day, man does not know the full depth of evil and will never know. But we now possess this knowledge, and we must become wise enough to know that we will and we can have victory over Satan's kingdom if we obey God. Satan has people fighting each other when they should be joining forces and fighting against him—the kingdom of darkness.

Genesis 2:16-17   And the Lord God commanded the man, saying of every tree of the garden thou mayest freely eat:

But of the tree of the knowledge of good and evil, thou shalt not eat of it: for in the day that thou eatest thereof thou shalt surely die.

There were three types of trees in the Garden of Eden, and they had the ability to produce after their kind. In the garden, there were the food trees, which consisted of edible things in fruit and plant form. The tree of life was in the midst of the garden; it was a symbol of the spirit, which is Jesus. And thirdly, the tree of knowledge of good and evil was in the garden. This tree was a representation that mankind eating thereof would surely cause death.

Genesis 2:9   And out of the ground made the Lord God to grow every tree that is pleasant to the sight, and good for food; the tree of life also in the midst of the garden, and the tree of knowledge of good and evil.

Genesis 2:16-17   And the Lord God commanded the man, saying, "You may freely eat of every tree of the garden; but of the tree of the knowledge of good and evil you shall not eat, for in the day that you eat of it you shall die."

In the day when God created a new heaven and a new earth, which means a new way of living, God made man from the dust of the same earth that produces the food trees, and he blew the breath of life into him. Man did not have the knowledge of good and evil in those days; he only had the knowledge of good and could only produce life. But because God made man in his likeness and in his image, man possesses the ability to choose—he has free will.

Genesis 1:26   And God said, let us make man in our image, after our likeness. And let them have dominion over the fish of the sea, and over the fowl of the air, and over the cattle, and over all the earth, and over every creeping thing that creepeth upon the earth.

Because of man's free will, God commanded him not to partake of the tree of knowledge of good and evil. This was a tree that had the ability to produce life and death, and God knew that the day man partook of the knowledge of this tree he would surely die.

How did this tree of knowledge of good and evil get into the garden? Once upon a time, when Jesus walked the land in flesh, he was teaching the people about discipleship. And he sent out seventy besides his disciples into the world to win the soul. They returned to him saying how the devil was subject to them in his name. Jesus answered them saying that he had beheld Satan as lightning falls from heaven. This event took place while Jesus was yet in heaven before he came to earth to become the Savior of the world.

The new heaven and new earth that are the new order were created because the first heaven and the first earth, which were the old order, had passed away due to the disobedience of man. God decided that he would create a new heaven and a new earth—a new way of living, a new way of thinking, and a new mind. To understand fully what God is doing, we have to think about when we ourselves are trying to make something perfect—how many times do we have to start over before we get it just right? This is what God is doing—he continues to start over trying to get creation back to its original state before the fall of Adam and Eve. This will happen when God is able to get the people to obey him.

Revelation 21:1   And I saw a new heaven and a new earth: for the first heaven and the first earth were passed away; and there was no more sea.

Now in the beginning when God created the heaven and the earth, everything he made was good. The creation of the heaven and the earth took place in the mind of God. He visualized everything before he made anything, and there is no evil in God. Man would have never had a problem if he had remained in the mind of God. It was not until God formed man out of the dust of the earth that he would come into contact with trouble.

Genesis 2:7   And the Lord God formed man of the dust of the ground, and breathed into his nostrils the breath of life; and man became a living soul.

Every commandment that is written is to protect man from some type of danger that will cause death. This danger may be physical, mental, or emotional. If we look back upon the presidential election in the year 2000, we can discern that something had to be urgent when manipulation and theft were said to have been involved in the highest office of a country. But if we for a moment take our minds off the president himself and look at the tree of knowledge of good and evil, we will capture another picture that will reveal what this tree of knowledge of good and evil is trying to accomplish. One thing that can clearly be seen is that death is involved. Therefore, we know that the thoughts are originating from a tree that can produce death, but why is this tree so interested in America? I believe the devil wants to destroy this country because this is the land flowing with milk and honey created by God to help others. The devil knows if he can cut off the source of help, the world will become vulnerable, and he will be in control. Look at how many people will become helpless if America comes to naught.

The true war is not a war between flesh and blood, it is a war between good and evil—God and the devil. The trick of the devil is to create a war between flesh and blood; this is the only way he has any chance at winning the war between himself and God. By separating the people, Satan can accomplish his mission because together we stand and divided we fall. These are the days when we need to take a good look at Satan and stop him from destroying our country, while acknowledging that there are people who need to be dealt with because people become vessels the devil uses to carry out his plans by choice. No matter what act of evil comes into existence, it originates in a place where there is disbelief in God's word and a willing vessel to be used.

If we take a moment and give this war some serious thought, we will find the root of the terrorism that concerns so many in the world today. If we only put aside our feelings toward others just for a moment to search for the origin of the terrorist, I believe we can truly identify him. And in doing so, we can rid our country and the world of terrorism and attain ceasefire. These are just a few measures that can be taken to begin the process of healing the world from terror. God drew the blueprint and man changed the plan, this is the reason for the state we are in today.

CHAPTER FIVE

THE ROOT OF ALL EVIL

The seed or the root of terrorism lies within each person in the world today. It is called sin. Satan the devil, our enemy, is the father of lies. And when he plants thoughts within the minds of the people that are contrary to the will of God and we accept these thoughts, they become sins. Sin is conceived by our desires, which originate from lust and enticement. Many times, we desire to do things that we should not or to have things that we should not, and we know this is true because the word of God speaks against such things. But we desire these things anyway.

When we accept the thought of doing and having such things, these thoughts open the door to the terrorist, and the devil provides us with a plan enabling the desires to come to pass. An example of this would be when someone desires to rob a bank; the devil will give the person a plan which will allow him to rob the bank. The plan may be workable or it may not be so workable, because it is given from a spirit of deception by the devil. The devil does not care whether the plan is successful or not; his job is to get you out of your relationship with God by causing disobedience to the word and creating a plane where he can work. Once he has created a plane where he can work, he is now able to create destruction using people as his agents. We cannot afford to forget that this war is between God and the devil; they are enemies, and they are at war against each other. Therefore, when a commandment is broken, the devil gains control and is able to bring destruction. We must fully understand that we are nothing more than agents, and we are either working for God or for the devil.

James 1:14-15   But every man is tempted, when he is drawn away of his own lust, and enticed. Then when lust hath conceived, it bringeth forth sin: and sin when it is finished, bringeth forth death.

John 10:10   The thief cometh not, but for to steal, and to kill, and to destroy: I am come that they might have life, and that they might have it more abundantly.

If we can remember that the battle is between God and the devil and it is over the soul of man, we can begin to heal our country. We can focus our attention on the problem—the devil. The devil wants man to die in sin and go to hell so he can get the soul. God wants man to live separate from sin. And when he departs from planet Earth, he goes to heaven, and God gets the soul. I hope these sayings help prepare us to better understand the war that is going on. This war is between good and evil, and we are nothing more than players in the game.

The good news about all this is there is a promise from God for doing good and a promise for doing evil. All we have to do is choose the side we want to play on. If we choose to be on God's side, we will receive the promises for doing good that are recorded in Deuteronomy 28:1-14 and eliminate destruction from our lives. If we choose to be on Satan's side, which is the devil, we will continue to receive the curses that are recorded in Deuteronomy 28:15-68 until we are totally destroyed.

If we the people desire peace in America, we must choose the Lord's side and return to the pillars and foundation that this country was built upon. Terror is much bigger than the president is or than any person is; this is the work of the enemy like we have never seen him before, and he is after as many souls as possible. Yes, there are people that the devil is using as agents in this war, but going after the people only will not get rid of this problem. We must go after the root of this problem, which is sin.

There is a story in the Bible where the servant of the Lord was at war as we are today. This story is recorded in the book of Joshua. It is one of the most interesting events in the Bible history because it reveals the solution to a problem that seemed to have no resolution. There is a statement recorded by Thomas Nelson that reveals it this way. He said, "Through three major military campaigns involving more than thirty enemy armies, the people of Israel learn a crucial lesson under Joshua's capable leadership. They learned that victory comes through faith in God and obedience to his word, rather than through military might or numerical superiority." During this time, Israel was at war with the Amorites, and they were winning against their enemy until one of the Israelites sinned; he took of the accursed thing, which God had commanded them not to take. Therefore, sin entered the camp, and Israel could no longer stand against their enemy. Words of wisdom: when sin enters into a situation, it removes the chance for resolution.

Joshua 7:11-12   Israel has sinned, and they have also transgressed my covenant, which I commanded them: for they have even taken of the accursed thing, and have also stolen, and dissemble also, and they have even put it among their own stuff.

Therefore the children of Israel could not stand before their enemies, but turned their backs before their enemies, because they were accursed: neither will I be with you any more, except you destroy the accursed from among you.

It does not matter how sin enters in, it will bring death and destruction as long as it is present. Many statements about the disasters in the world today have been made. People just cannot understand why these things are happening. But I will tell you this: where there is so much calamity in the world it is because of sin and sin only. God loves his people, and there is only one thing that will tie his hands from helping his people—and that is sin. In the scriptures above, Joshua 7:11-12, you can see how observant and detailed God is. Look at how he describes to Joshua the sin of Israel: he is paying close attention to what is going on. This lets me know that when things happen, it is because of sin, which is the only thing that will tie up the hands of God even though he is watching so closely.

One of the most troubling statements I have read in the word of God was recorded in the twelfth verse of the passage above, when God said that because of sin, "neither will I be with you anymore, except you destroy the accursed from among you." God is bothered by sin so much because it is the only thing that will not allow him to protect his people. Do you think God is upset with America because the sin that is within her? Can he be saying to America, you have sinned, and I am no longer with you?

This is frightening to know, but sin will always separate the people from God. Satan knows this, and he is doing everything he can to keep the people sinning to keep on separating them from God. As long as he can keep the people sinning, Satan is in control to do whatsoever he desires: it may be death or destruction. This is an open opportunity for the devil to win the soul of people. It cannot be said enough that it is the soul of man that the devil is after and nothing else. Everything he is doing is to put man in a position where he has a chance of winning his soul.

So if we hate the devil as much as we say we do, we should be running to Jesus as fast as we can so that we can be equipped to fight against Satan. Satan is skillful, cunning, and crafty, and he is good at using the word of God against the people of God. Therefore, if we do not know what God is saying in his word, Satan has the upper hand. It does not matter what the enemy tries to do to us. As long as we are keeping the commandment, we are protected. Because the word of God is a shield for us, and the enemy can only attack where sin is present.

Speaking concerning the war in Iraq, Satan does not care about the Americans or the Iraqis; he has put a plan in motion that will cause death, and his desire is that someone dies in sin. So it is up to us the people to know better. We have Jesus and the written word so how could we allow the devil to get us in a situation like this? You know what Satan did? He used that which is unknown to us as a weapon against us.

Hosea 4:6   My people are destroyed for lack of knowledge: because thou hast rejected knowledge, I will also reject thee, that thou shalt be no priest to me: seeing thou hast forgotten the law of thy God, I will also forget thy children.

People all over the world today are being destroyed for the lack of knowledge. I will reject those who reject knowledge, and they will not be a priest to me. This is the word of the Lord recorded in Hosea 4:6. Even the children are forgotten because of the rejection of knowledge, and we wonder what is wrong with our youth today.

This is a lethal weapon in the hands of the devil. As long as Satan can keep people ignorant of the word of God, he will control the people, doing whatever evil he desires. It has been often said that knowledge is power, and this statement is proving itself to be true. If we do not learn the word of God for ourselves, then let's do it for the children and for our loved ones. Are we so soon to forget 9/11, the Columbine massacre, the Washington DC sniper, the Oklahoma bombing, kidnapping, child molestation, gang activity, gay and lesbian rights, the Nicole Simpson and Ron Goldman murders, the war in Iraq, the tsunamis, AIDS, hunger, homelessness, fires, and earthquakes, just to name a few?

America should never forget what the lack of knowledge has done, because we are a nation built upon the word of God. We must remember that sin allows bad things to enter creation. Thinking that the crime is over after an evil act has taken place and the offender has been caught and charged is anything but true. If the offense is murder and you capture and punish the person who committed the murder, the crime is not over, because the devil will find another offender and continue to kill.

We must get to the root of this problem in America, and we must do it now. I have written this book to reveal to you the things that God has revealed to me—the cunning craftiness of the devil and the power that sin has over creation. This enemy has been pulling stunts from the beginning of time. He did the same thing to Adam and Eve in the Garden of Eden when he deceived them into believing something that was not true. Now that God has revealed to us the cunning craftiness of the devil, we can no longer sit still and do nothing, we must fight a good fight against our adversary. And we must win this battle over sin. We must turn back to the word of God because it will be by the word of God that we will destroy the enemy in America and other parts of the world.

There are so many people in the world today who reject the gospel of Jesus Christ simply because they do not understand the importance of knowing Christ. Can we for a moment think that God will send his only begotten son to the cross to die for our sins, and not hold us accountable for not receiving salvation? God forbid. There is a price to pay for disobeying God's command, and the enemy knows this, and he uses it as a weapon to attack and to destroy mankind.

Deuteronomy 28:1-2   And it shall come to pass, if thou shalt hearken diligently unto the voice of the Lord thy God, to observe and to do all his commandments which I command thee this day, that the Lord thy God will set thee on high above all nations of the earth:

And all these blessings shall come on thee, and overtake thee, if thou shalt hearken unto the voice of the Lord thy God.

Deuteronomy 28:15   But it shall come to pass, if thou wilt not hearken unto the voice of the Lord thy God, to observe to do all his commandments and his statutes which I command thee this day; that all these curses shall come upon thee, and overtake thee.

Everything that is to be known pertaining to life is written in the word of God along with all the dos and don'ts. But to know these things, we must read the Bible, attend church, or go to Bible school so we can learn what God is saying. The world is perishing because of what we do not know, not because of what we know. Right now at this time the enemy has the upper hand in America; he knows that we lack knowledge of the word, and he is using our lack to his advantage. Satan will not attack where the word of God is believed; he is no match for the word of God. It is the powerful thing in creation, and he knows this. There is nothing on earth that is more powerful than the word of God.

Matthew 5:18   For verily I say unto you, Till heaven and earth pass, one jot or one tittle shall in no wise pass from the law, till all be fulfilled.

Matthew 24:34-35   Verily I say unto you, This generation shall not pass, till all these things be fulfilled. Heaven and earth shall pass away, but my words shall not pass away.

We must understand who Satan is. Once upon a time he was the archangel of God; his name was Lucifer, meaning son of the morning. His job was to sing praises and usher in the morning. He lived with God, but he was kicked out of heaven because he desired to exalt himself above God. While living with God,

Satan knew God. He knows his likes and his dislikes better than man does. Man will never be able to win a war against the devil without help from God. This is why God emphasizes keeping the commandments so much. He knew that when

Lucifer was cast out of heaven into earth, he would make war with the inhabitants of the earth. But Lucifer the devil has no power over mankind as long as man keeps the commandments. We as a nation must understand that we cannot do anything without the word of God. So many times we think that we do not need God, but this is nothing but another one of Satan's deceptions.

John 5:30   I can of mine own self do nothing: as I hear, I judge: and my judgement is just; because I seek not mine own will, but the will of the Father which hath sent me.

2 Corinthians 13:8   For we can do nothing against the truth, but for the truth.

We cannot prevail against the devil without help from God, and we cannot receive help from God if we are in sin. Sin will keep us separated from God, and obedience to God's word will draw us closer to him. And it will produce success, it will provide protection and whatever we need at any given time. But how can anything that is not known be done? Wisdom, knowledge, and understanding are the keys to life's success. But anything that is not known cannot be done, and the things that are to be understood have been made known to us. These things that are known come from the wisdom of God.

CHAPTER SIX

UNDERSTANDING GOD

Understanding God is an important factor in building a strong and successful nation, community, or person. If everyone would do their part to fulfill the will of God in their personal life, building a strong community that would build a strong nation and then a strong world would be auspicious. Whether it is the success of a nation, a community, or an individual, there are some godly truths that have been put into action in order for the success to take place. One thing must be understood—that is, we are all part of the body of Christ. We may not all be in Christ or have the mind of Christ, but God has created everyone. And we all live in the same world, and whether we are good or bad, we have influence on the earth in which we live.

Getting an understanding of how all human bodies work as one is essential. Studying the operation of our individual body will help us to understand how our bodies work together as a nation. For example, if we learn how each member of the human body contributes to the operation of the body, it will give clarity about how things are created to work on the earth. There are many types of human bodies: we have the individual body of Christ, which consists of one person. Then it extends to the family, the church, the town, the city, the county, the state, and the country. All these are part of the body of Christ, which is made up of more than one member or more than one person.

Likewise, the natural body is made up of more than one member. And all the members working together will allow an individual to do the things they do. If any member of our individual body such as the heart becomes ill, the body will not perform in the same manner as if there was no illness. Sickness that is in the world, which is made up of all people in creation, is known as sin. And it has the same effect on the world as sickness that is within the body. For example, if same-sex relations are considered cancer, this can easily become a major problem within the country because we know what cancer does to the individual body.

Now sin rages on two different levels: there is an individual level of sin, and there is a corporate level of sinning. The individual level of sin consists of one person committing the sin, and that person will be held responsible for the sin committed, and all punishment will fall upon that individual. If the sin is on the corporate level, it means that more than one individual is involved, and the corporate body will be held accountable for the sin. To avoid this type of sinning is important for all members of the world to understand how this level of sin works. It takes place when there are leaders incorporated, and they represent all members of the body. Sin comes into play after a commandment is broken, and a commandment must be broken for it to be a sin. All the members of the corporate body are in agreement with the decision, whether the decision was made directly or indirectly. This is a corporate sin, and it will bring a corporate destruction. If the leader is a pastor, then the church will pay the price for the sin. If the leader is the mayor, the city will pay for the sin. If the leader is the governor, then the state will pay for the sin. If the leader is the president of the country, then the country will pay the price for the sin.

Corporate sin opens the door for destruction in any area represented by the leader. This is the number one reason why everyone should vote. It is important that everyone of legal age has a voice in who is elected as leader because that person will represent everyone as a whole, and they will represent the people before man and God. We are not only held accountable for keeping man's law, but we are held accountable for keeping God's laws, which are the commandments. Therefore, when we choose a leader, a quality that should always be desired is their faith in God. A person who is affiliated with man's law and God's law makes the best leader. Faith leaders are less likely to transgress the commands of God because they know if they do God's will, it will hold them more accountable, because it is better not to know than to know and not do.

Congressmen should always be people of great faith because they are responsible for the laws that govern the country; these laws must not transgress the laws of God. If a law is put into effect that works against the law of God, this will put the country in a vulnerable state because God's law is higher than man's law. Now this transgression can become a weapon for the enemy because everyone is required to obey the law. If a law is put in place that defies the law of God and the people are keeping this law, the whole region becomes vulnerable to calamity. Therefore carefully selecting leaders is important because once they have been sworn into office, they become the representative of the people before God and man; it is the same as if we the people were standing before God.

Not only America, but the world has forgotten about God's involvement on earth. We no longer realize that we are accountable to God, and he judges our deeds according to his word. Continuing our daily activities as though we will not be held accountable by God is a dangerous lifestyle, and tragedy can present itself anywhere and at any time. Everyone is talking about freedom, but what is freedom? It is the opportunity to live a lifestyle free from the bondage of sin. It is not an opportunity for sin to prevail such as has taken place in the world today. This kind of lifestyle is not freedom; it is bondage like we have never seen.

Proverbs 14:34   Righteousness exalteth a nation: but sin is a reproach to any people.

America and other nations of the world have sinned, and there is an accursed thing among all the people. This accursed thing is sin, and it has many faces. Finding these accursed things and getting rid of them is a mission that every nation needs to accomplish. But what is it that is so displeasing to God? Something that he has commanded us not to do, and we have disobeyed him. We must turn to the Bible and search the scriptures to find the truth, and when we have found the truth, we must be truthful to ourselves and obey the word of God. There are things that are an abomination to God, and we have become partakers of these things also.

Abomination to God is cutting off the Messiah, which is Jesus the word of God. It means to pretend the word of God does not exist even after the word is proven to be true. These abominable things take place not only in America but all over the world. Yet while knowing that the word of God speaks against these things, we participate in doing them anyway. Here is the truth we all need to know; that is, if the enemy cuts off the word of God, he will be able to take over America. Therefore, we must give some serious thoughts to the things we are doing because if we continue in disobedient behavior, there is nothing for God to do but to leave man to destroy himself. God has given man dominion over the earth, and he is not going to take it from man. In the days of Noah, when God allowed the earth to be destroyed by the flood, man was sinning like he is sinning today. So now God is speaking to us again, trying to warn us that if we do not stop disobeying the commandments doing all these abominable things, we can easily bring upon ourselves something that will destroy us today. God said that he will not destroy the earth with water again, and we know this is true because the rainbow is a sign of this covenant between God and man concerning the flood. But what scares me is that it has been said that the earth will be destroyed by fire, and when I think of nuclear weapons, I think of fire.

For this reason, I am writing this message that God is revealing to me so the people will know what is happening in the world today. What is taking place with what is known as weapons of mass destruction is nothing more than the work of the devil allowed by God, and if God is allowing something, it cannot be stopped by flesh and blood. I cannot say that there are weapons of mass destruction being created or not, but what I can say is that there is nothing hidden that is not going to be revealed. Therefore, I can only prepare the minds of people to the intention of the devil, our enemy, to destroy the world with permission from God. We do not want something to come upon us unawares, and if there are people participating in behavior of this sort, building weapons to destroy others, they have no idea that the same weapons are going to destroy them too.

I know some may not understand what is being said in this writing, but we must understand that people are not the enemy—the devil is the enemy. Until we understand this, we will always be fighting a losing battle in fighting each other. Think about this, God created people. Do you think that his intention was to create something to destroy his creation? No, God created people of every nation to become his family, and every nation represents a different child in his sight with a different talent. Look at the children you have; they do not have the same talent. The only difference between God and us is that we only need one person to have a child where God needs many persons to make one child. Within our body, one cell begins our life. In God, the body of one person is equal to one cell. Whenever there is a disagreement between people, always look for the influence of the devil and do not be afraid or be ashamed to ask for help. Never let the devil cause you to bring harm to another human being; they are your sisters or your brothers, and we are all God's children. Let us not forget the incidents in the school system. It should always be an example for us. We know what happened when the enemy took prayer—the word of God—out of the schools.

Mark 13:14   But when you shall see the abomination of desolation, spoken of by Daniel the Prophet, standing where it ought not (let him that readeth understand) then let them that are in Judaea flee to the mountains.

The Bible tells us that when we see the abomination of desolation standing where it ought not to be, we should fly to the mountains. This means that when we see the word of God being cut off or taken away, run for your life because desolation, which is sudden destruction, is near. Sudden destruction comes without a warning;

it appears when the word of God has been removed. God is our defense, he is our protector; and when we allow the word of God to be present, he is present.

John 1:1   In the beginning was the Word, and the Word was with God, and the Word was God.

If we look at marriages of the same sex by looking at the sin—not the people—we see a sin that has the ability to cause great destruction. Why? Because it is an abomination to God. It is an insult to God as if what he did was not good enough. Meaning, that something has been added to creation that God did not create. If we read in the generations of the heaven and of the earth in the book of Genesis chapter 2, we will not find same-sex marriages in there. I chose this particular sin because this is an area where Satan desires to keep us ignorant. He wants our eyes to remain closed to the word of God concerning this matter. But we must address this particular sin because God said that if we add anything to his creation, he would add to us the plagues written in his word. We must remember that God hated same-sex sin so much that in the Old Testament days when man was under the law God allowed two whole cities to be destroyed because of the behavior. Today cities are being destroyed and I wonder what sin is causing the calamity.

Knowing that sin is the only thing that can bring about this type of calamity upon the earth is vital information we should all be aware of. The word of God teaches us that everything God has made is good, and God made man. Therefore I believe that God who hates same-sex behavior will not create people in this manner. But what I do believe is that something is happening within the mind that is not the will of God, and it needs to be addressed. There are some people today who still believe in the Old Testament law, which allowed stoning people to death because of sin. But we know that Jesus Christ the Savior of the world has come already, and his reason for coming was to redeem us from the curse of the law. Thus, people are no longer stoned to death for sin. But if we pause for a moment we can ask ourselves the question, Why did the people in the days of the old stone people to death for sin? The answer to this question will reveal the importance of getting rid of sin. In the days of old, they stoned people who sinned because they knew that sin would bring calamity upon all the people. Therefore, to avoid destruction, they would stone to death everyone who sinned. But after the coming of Jesus Christ, stoning itself became a sin. So to kill someone because of a sin is a sinful act and, therefore, is punishable by law. So now we must learn the ways of God through his word, which will save us from destruction; it is the only way we can overcome sin.

Whenever I use the word overcome, I think about the great Dr. Martin Luther King Jr. saying, "We shall overcome someday." To this day, I do not believe we the people understood what he was saying. Because many questions have risen since his speech, people have wondered whether his prediction will ever come to pass. But I believe that Dr. King was speaking about sin because overcoming sin is the only thing that will set men free, not overcoming racism. If we overcome sin, racism will die, gang banging will die, and murdering and all other evil acts will die. When Jesus died on the cross—most of us have seen The Passion of Christ by Mel Gibson—it happened so that we can overcome sin. If he had not died and become the Savior of the world, stoning would be legal today. It would be lawful to stone a person to death for their sins. This stoning gives me an idea of just how bad sin is.

But I do not want to confuse anyone into thinking that God hates people, because this is not true. God does not hate people; he hates their sins. His hatred for sin is because sin is the only thing Satan has that he can use against the people and disable God from doing anything about it. Can you imagine something that would keep you from coming to your child's defense when they are in trouble and in need of your help? This is the position sin put God in, and it is the only thing that keeps him from coming to our rescue when we are in trouble. The devil is God's enemy; he is attacking God's children, and God cannot do anything about it because he cannot go against his own word. If God goes against his word, he will be going against himself—he will no longer be God.

When people ask why God allows tragedy, this is the answer: our sin leaves God no other choice. This is why God tells us to keep his commandments. I hope you are beginning to understand God a little more. So can you imagine how God our Heavenly Father feels when he is put in a position where he cannot come to the rescue of his own children? I know this has to be unbearable for him. Sometimes I just sit and weep when I see bad things happening. I know the people just do not understand what is taking place. This is why from the very moment we repent of our sins, the situation begins to change. The situation changes because God comes on the scene, and he has been patiently waiting for an opportunity to give the devil a black eye for messing with us.

Under the New Testament law, Jesus redeemed men from the curse of the law, and we have a God-given opportunity to repent. And God will not allow destruction to come without giving a warning and without giving a chance for repentance. So do not miss the warning signs; always look for God in a situation. If you are reading this book, consider it a warning sign about sin and repentance.

Now that we have some knowledge and understanding about God and how his kingdom operates, we can begin the healing process. Every human being in creation should know this knowledge so that they can outline their own life and not the devil. When we look at the world system, it operates somewhat like God's kingdom; therefore, we can learn more about God from this system. In the world when a law is broken, there are already written laws that give full instruction about the punishment for breaking that law. An example of a law that can be broken in the world system would be not obeying a traffic light or a stop sign. In God's kingdom, the same principle applies. There are already written laws that have been set down thousands of years ago giving full instructions for the punishment for breaking a command. The difference between a law of the world and a command of God is the punishment. The world uses the term law meaning it can be changed, and God uses the term command meaning it is eternal—it cannot be changed. But because there is a lack of knowledge concerning the purpose of the commands of God and the laws of God, the people suffer many unnecessary things.

To learn the laws of the world, we need to access the law library or go to law school. To become knowledgeable in the laws and commands of God, we need to read the Bible. There is a lack of interest in reading the Bible, and I believe this is because it has not yet been made fully known how important the word of God is. What Jesus did on Calvary cross was to redeem us from the curse of the law so we do not have to be stoned to death for our sins and wrongdoings—we can repent. Now the curse of the law is the punishment for breaking a command, and because it is a command, the punishment will not change; therefore, it is always best to repent of the sin and the wrongdoing. So what Jesus did on the cross has moved men from under the curse of the law to under the grace of God. Now, when we sin, we have a time to repent before the punishment comes. So today, we do not have to live by the law; we can live by grace because we can repent for any sin or wrongdoing we have committed.

The problem comes when we do not repent. When we do not repent, we slowly begin to move back under the law that we have been redeemed from, and the law brings death. It is as if Jesus's death was in vain. We have not yet been consumed because we have a chance to repent and get things right with God. Now repentance does not consist of saying I am sorry only, it also means turning away from the sinful act and never doing it again.

We need to be educated about grace because it is essential for repentance. When we sin, if we do not repent, destruction will come because it will be as though we reject the gift of God and say we would rather live by way of the law. It is crucial that we understand God because we can get into a lot of trouble simply by our ways and our actions. We do not have to speak a word to get into trouble. This one thing we must learn: that our God cannot be taken advantage of, tricked, nor can he be manipulated like man. Therefore, once we realize sin has taken place, repentance and restitution must follow because we have entered into grace. Grace is the time given by God to correct the wrongdoing and turn from the sin. If the grace expires before true repentance comes, it can possibly end in death.

Now grace is the undeserved favor of God; it serves as a covering or a shelter. This is the area where most people fall short concerning God's promises. Grace is not the favor of God; it is the undeserved favor of God, meaning you do not deserve this. God gives this to you out of his loving-kindness. So we must continue on in God until we reach the favor of God—meaning, that we deserve the things we are receiving because of our obedience to his word. Therefore, we now understand what God was saying when he said, if any man is in Christ Jesus he is a new creation. So all the putting on of the new man and the putting off of the old man is nothing more than becoming a new creation.

Romans 6:14   For sin shall not have dominion over you: for ye are not under the law, but under grace.

Now concerning repentance, this decision is controlled by God. He knows who is truly overcoming sin. People who are not born again are under grace; this means that there is a time set by God for repentance to take place before death or destruction occurs. We have to remember that when sin is in control, there is no covering or protection; the only thing that is present is grace, which is the undeserved favor of God serving as a temporary covering until the true covering comes. Think about it this way: what have you had in your life that was temporary? Something that you had use of only until the real thing came. For example, some car insurance will allow you to use a rental car until your original car is repaired. Once your original car is repaired, you no longer have access to the rental car even though it still exists. Meaning that the rental car was only temporary.

Now what do you think will happen when grace expires? Even though grace is eternal, death and destruction can come if you do nothing with the grace that God gives you. This is just something to think about when we do not take God seriously. When we do not take the gift of God seriously and repent of our sins.

Think about this: if Jesus Christ had not come, there would be no repentance. You think the conditions of the world are not good now. Without Jesus and repentance, it would be even worse. And if we do not begin to repent, it is going to become as if Jesus Christ had never come.

I thank God for being God because even when we are in sin, he gives us grace until true change comes. If the devil had his way, we would not have grace; the world would already be destroyed by now because his desire is that all those who sin be destroyed without any opportunity to change. But thanks be unto our God who knows all things and has sent his only begotten son into the world, and by his death has given grace to his people.

Nevertheless, we cannot take advantage of God's grace because death or destruction will surely come. After continually rejecting the call of God for repentance no one is allowed to continue in wrongdoing. There is a turning point—as Tyrone Davis would say, I reached the turning point, Lord, Lord in my life. So there is a turning point for all things, and for sin death is at the end, so let us make haste and repent. Many gospel ministers have said that many people die before their time. This has been proven to be a true statement, and it signifies why becoming born again is so important, and why repentance is so powerful.

Knowing what sin is and the power and control it has over our lives is essential so repentance can be understood. True repentance cannot take place until what sin is and what sin does have been revealed. To know what things are sinful and what things are not sinful must be learned from the word of God. The local churches and synagogues play an important role in this matter. They are responsible for teaching the truth concerning God's word. They are responsible for revealing, making known, and exposing sin, preaching and teaching the word so that healing can take place in the land. Healing will never happen as long as sin is present, and Satan cannot cast Satan out. Sin is like cancer; it must be destroyed or it will continue to eat away until it causes death. But when sin is made known, there is no longer an excuse for continued sinning. To do so will release the curses for sinning that are written in the book of the law. If sin has not been made known or exposed, the churches and the synagogues are failing the people.

Isaiah 58:1   Cry aloud, spare not, lift up thy voice like a trumpet, and show my people their transgression, and the house of Jacob their sins.

Now to continue in sin after it has been revealed causes one to be removed from God's temporary protection and covering, which is his mercy and grace. There is no one who wants to be without the mercy and grace of God, that would be a state of no return. But when we make the Lord our shepherd, goodness and mercy will follow us all the days of our life. Think of the Israelites in the book of Joshua, who disobeyed God after he warned them in detail what things should not be taken from the enemy because they were accursed things. They lost their covering and protection due to disobedience. There came a time during a battle with the Amorites when the Israelites were unable to stand. They began to lose the battle and had to flee before the enemy. Joshua their leader became so discouraged because he did not know why the Israelites were being defeated and some were getting killed—this was God's army. But he knew something had caused the Israelites to lose the covering and protection of God. God had promised to be with them as long as they obeyed his commandments. The enemy began prevailing over the Israelites, so much so that Joshua rent his garment, fell upon his face on the ground, and cried out to God, saying, "Wherefore has thou brought this people over Jordan to be delivered into the hands of the Amorites." God replied to Joshua, "Get up, Israel has sinned."

It may not be known today precisely what sin is causing certain destruction, but we do know this: that it is because of sin. When we transgress the commands of God and take part in things that are accursed, these things will become a snare unto the people. Accursed things are things that are abomination to God. Abominable things are things that God hates because his word has been presented as meaningless or void as though he had not spoken. They are the things that take away or add to the word of God. These are things that will cause people to fall prey to the enemy; therefore, the word of God must always be obeyed.

Matthew 5:17-18   Think not that I am come to destroy the law, or the prophets: I am not come to destroy, but to fulfil.

For verily I say unto you, till heaven and earth pass, one jot or one tittle shall in no wise pass from the law, till all is fulfilled.

We have to become wise because the devil knows the importance of obeying the word of God; he knows what will happen if the word of God is not kept. He has a strategy of going to and fro on the earth watching to see what commandments are being broken and who he can devour. He watches believers more than others to see who is breaking the commandment; these are easy prey, for they profess to obey the word. After successfully finding a target, the devil moves in for the kill. This is the method that Bin Laden is trying to use to get control of America. Bin Laden has done his research. He knows that the word of God is the foundation on which America was built upon. Think about this: if you take away the foundation of something, what will happen to the thing? This is Bin Laden's method; he is trying to take away what America believes in, and his source is the devil.

The devil targets the believer; he goes before God accusing the believers of not obeying the commands, reminding God of his written punishment for disobedience. This gives the devil access to the person. He cannot just attack someone; he has to have legal grounds. And reminding God what command is broken gives him legal ground. It is no different than being in a court of law standing before a judge and being found guilty for a crime. The next step the judge takes is to sentence you to jail. This is what takes place when the devil accuses a person before God. If you are found guilty of what the devil is saying, he gains access to you. The devil knows the word of God. He is so evil he will not stop at this point. He goes on to try to convince God that even those who are obedient will turn from believing in him if he takes away certain privileges. This is a test that Job, in the Bible, had to endure. What can God do in a situation like this? He cannot go against his own words. If he does, he will no longer be God.

What I am saying is that we have an enemy working against God and against us. God is not requiring his people to obey the commandments just to have something to do. We must understand that our well-being and the well-being of our children depends upon our obedience to God's word. Satan knows the vulnerabilities of people; he makes this determination based upon what commandments are being broken. Satan watches us more than we watch him, but God told us in his word that he also watches us, and we have to pray. So we can clearly see that this is a war between good and evil.

Matthew 26:41   Watch and pray that ye enter not into temptation: the spirit indeed is willing, but the flesh is weak

God is spirit and Satan is a spirit too. Therefore, we must learn how to watch for open doors that can be used by the enemy for an entrance into our life. Having other gods before our God is an open door for the enemy. This is one of the first commands God gave the people when he delivered them from the house of bondage: have no other God before me.

Exodus 20:3 and 6-9   Thou shalt have no other gods before me Thou shalt not make unto thee any graven image, or any likeness of any thing that is in heaven above, or that is in the earth beneath, or that is in the water under the earth:

Thou shalt not bow down thyself to them, nor serve them: for I the Lord thy God am a jealous God, visiting the iniquity of the fathers upon the children unto the third and fourth generation of them that hate me;

> And showing mercy unto thousands of them that love me, and keep my commandments.

We can see how detailed God is. His request was not only to have no other gods before him, he revealed what other gods may consist of. This is one of the sins that will produce death if its practice is continued. Same-sex relationship is another sin that produces death if its practice is continued. Here again God says that a man should leave his father and mother and cleave (be joined) to his wife (his woman) and the twain (two) shall become one. When we operate outside of these God-given principles, we add to the word of God. The word did not tell us to do anything else when it comes to marriage.

Following the scriptures is the best thing to do if we are in dispute about what is right or wrong. Simply look it up in the word and see what God is saying about your concerns. There are books in the bookstores that are good references to help you find whatever you need to know about in the Bible. If you cannot find something in the word, then it is not the will of God. It cannot be found anywhere in the scriptures where God told a man to marry a man or a woman to marry a woman. To do this is to add something to the word of God, and this is not good.

Revelation 22:18 For I testify unto every man that heareth the words of the prophecy of this book, If any man add unto these things, God shall add unto him the plagues that are written in this book:

And if any man shall take away of this prophecy, God shall take away his part out of the book of life, and out of the holy city and from the things which are written in this book.

If we really want to know why AIDS and all these incurable diseases have entered into creation, they are plagues. These are indeed critical times in creation, and this is a message that should be heard by everyone. We can no longer allow ourselves to fall prey to the devil by continuing to disobey the commands of God. We can no longer allow our innocent children, who have not yet had an opportunity to live life, to pay the price for sin. The price is too great and too costly, young people are dying in wars of every kind, paying for sin they had no part in. It is time for the truth to be told in America and the world. Now is the time to take a stand against sin at all costs. No longer can any nation of people tolerate sin, because the whole world has already experienced what sin can do if it is not cut off the minute it exposes its ugly head.

Can we just continue to go along with the program, knowing that the program is working against the will of God? There is no room for compromising our young people, who have just become adults, have not yet learned what life is all about, but are finding themselves defending countries who have not allowed their people to live. They have just become of age to learn what life is, and instead they are dying in wars whose root is sin. People all over the world are dying in disasters created by sin. It is time for the people of the world to stand up and say no more: no more to unrighteous governments, no more to the devil, and no more to all who are listening. We will not tolerate sin anymore. We will not pay the price for decisions based upon sin.

But how can we avoid paying for the sins of sinners? We do this when we refuse to take part in or uphold wrongdoing. All sin is against the commands of God, and the law is the punishment for breaking a command. Marriages of the same sex, serving strange gods, racism, and discrimination are against the laws of God. It is just as wrong as murdering, kidnapping, child molestation, pornography, lying, and stealing. It is just as bad as adultery, fornication, uncleanness, lewdness, idolatry, sorcery, witchcraft, hatred, contention, jealousies, anger, selfish ambitions, dissensions, heresies, envy, drunkenness, revelry, and gang activity. We cannot make wrong right no matter what way we turn it, and we cannot make God change his mind concerning his commandments. If we commit transgression, we need to repent quickly. If we cover it up, rest assured it will come to the light, and we will have to pay a price for it.

There was an old saying years ago when I was a child growing up. I would often hear an elder say it to a child who had done wrong and when asked about it would lie. The elder would say to the child, "You may have gotten by, but you have not gotten away." I have found this to be true for the people of the world today who have involved themselves in covering up a wrongdoing. They may get by, but they have not gotten away.

Luke 8:17   For nothing is secret that shall not be made manifest; neither any thing hid, that shall not be known and come abroad.

Numbers 23:19   God is not a man that he should lie; neither the son of man, that he should repent: hath he said, and shall he not do it? Or hath he spoken, and shall he not make it good?

Realizing this will cause the fear of God to enter people; it has scared me straight. I have had to take a few deep breaths, because if God speaks a word and does not bring it to pass, this means that he is no longer God. So whatever God says is coming to pass, and as a nation, we cannot be in agreement with things that we know are against the commands of God. Obedience to the laws of the land is just as important, as long as they are not contrary to the commands of God. In the world system if a person is with someone who breaks the law, the person becomes an accomplice and will be punished the same as if they had committed the crime.

James 4:7   Submit yourselves therefore to God. Resist the devil, and he will flee from you.

We cannot have anything to do with wrongdoing. The devil who is the thief comes to do three things according to the scripture:

John 10:10   The thief comes not, but for to steal, and to kill, and to destroy: I am come that they might have life, and that they might have it more abundantly.

Therefore, anytime there is stealing, killing, or destruction taking place, it is the work of the devil. Sin opens the door that invites the enemy to enter into our lives. So we have to be vigilant always, looking for acts that will lead to stealing, killing, and destruction. Closing every door to the enemy can mean the difference between life and death. If any area is observed where the enemy has crept in, taking time to identify the sin that allows the enemy entrance and closing the door through prayer and repentance is important; it could mean the difference between life and death. Sin is always the thing that is working against the command of God, so identify it and search for the root. The root is the lifeline, and it stems from lust or enticement of one's desires.

James 1:14-15   But every man is tempted, when he is drawn away of his own lust, and enticed.

                      Then when lust has conceived, it bringeth forth sin: and sin, when it is finished, bringeth forth death.

After the root has been discovered, destroy it in prayer and repentance. Remember, if an attempt to get rid of the problem is made without destroying the root, the problem will always return. It is not enough to call the cops when a crime is being committed, prayer is also necessary because the cops may catch the criminal, but they cannot catch the sin. Therefore, the sinful spirit just jumps from one person to another and keeps on committing crime.

It is also helpful to talk with others about problems and ask for help in praying. Invite God into your affairs, this will always produce a blessed outcome. It is so sad that so many lives have to be lost before society can come to the realization that something is wrong with the way things are being done. I look at how many students and faculty members became a statistic before society realized what the problem was in the schools. I do believe that this is a hard subject to talk about, but I also believe there are some things that must be addressed if we as a people are going to overcome today's fears. If prayer had remained in the school system, I do believe the tragedies that have taken place in the schools would not have happened. I say this because looking through the eyes of God, I realize that it is not what we know that causes us to perish, it is what we do not know.

Hosea 4:6   My people are destroyed for lack of knowledge: because thou hast rejected knowledge, I will also reject thee, that thou shalt be no priest to me: seeing thou hast forgotten the law of thy God, I will also forget thy children.

The word of God is God, and he is our covering and our protection. If you remove the word, you remove God. And when you remove God, the covering and protection are gone. Failure is what we as a nation have done. We have failed our young people because our job is to protect and to bring them up in the ways of God. Not only did we fail our young people, also we have deceived ourselves. How can we teach that which we have no knowledge of, and how can we practice that which we do not preach? Our greatest need is to return to God through his word so acts like these will never be repeated. When we return to God in obeisance to his word, I believe that God will return to us the lifestyle we once knew.

Galatians 6:7   Be not deceived; God is not mocked: for whatsoever a man soweth, that shall he also reap.

Sinning is the problem in America, and countries all over the world, I cannot say it enough. We all have sinned and fallen short of God's glory, but charity begins at home, and we are responsible for the bloodshed of the innocent in America. It is time for us to begin cleaning up this mess we have made. I believe we are no longer in a compromising position with God, we are in a stage of do or die. I believe that if we judge falsely, it brings harm to others and causes innocent bloodshed. Here we are today in 2007 and still dealing with the war in Iraq, another killing of young people trying to get rid of a problem by cutting off the branches. We will never get rid of a problem until the root has been found and destroyed. I often wonder if we will ever learn or what will it take to bring us to our right mind. For some sad reason, it seems that we think we can do things without the help of God. This country was founded on the word of God—it is the foundation. If the foundation is removed, what will make the country whole? What will stabilize it, support, or even protect it? How many lambs have to be sacrificed before we realize Jesus was the last sacrifice? America, do you not know that Jesus gave his life so we could live, not die?

Oh, ministers of the Most High God, is there a word from the Lord? It is time for America and the world to know who our God is, and what he will do for those who obey him. It was never the plan of God for America to come to the place in which it now stands. Do we not know that America is the land that the forefathers saw from afar, the land flowing with milk and honey? We are living in the land talked about so many years ago. Our job is to preserve this land and teach other nations the ways of our God so they too can live in the prosperity of our God. How can we do these things, which God has created us to do, when we partake of sin as if we have no God?

Sin should never be tolerated in America in the magnitude that it is presenting itself. If someone desires to sin, then let him sin, and upon his head will be the punishment required. The government officials and those in leadership should never tolerate nor have any input in anything that is an abomination to God; it is they who represent the people. If the government officials allow sinful behavior in a country, they will bring a curse upon the country, and all the people are opening a door for the enemy to attack. The first thing that takes place when tragedy occurs is we run to God asking why, Lord? But God did not open the door to the enemy; we did when we disobeyed his command. God has given us a way to keep the enemy out, but it is up to us to accept his way. We have already been forewarned what will happen if we break the commandments.

The problem is not that we have not heard, because we know about the Bible. We may not know what is in it because we have not read it. But we do know that it exists. We have to understand that the commandments are God's way of protecting us from our enemy. We have an enemy who wants all of us to die in sin, and he is killing as many as he can. But if we keep the commandments, no weapon that is formed against us can be used.

Isaiah 54:17   No weapon that is formed against thee shall prosper; and every tongue that shall rise against thee in judgement thou shalt condemn. This is the heritage of the servants of the Lord, and their righteousness is of me, saith the Lord.

We have been given all the information we need to know. So where is the information? It is upon the shelves of our home, in the stores, the library, churches, even in the hotels and motels. It is called the Bible. We have to return to God. We have to find time to read his words. I hope that in reading this book you will receive something that will cause you to want to become closer to God and read the Bible. After this, who can we blame for the problems in America now? We all are at fault, from the presidents of companies to housewives, from the president of the United States to the bum in the street. Where do we go from here? The process begins with each of us. We must search our individual hearts to see where sin lies within each one of us.

CHAPTER SEVEN

ARE YOUR SINS KILLING AMERICA?

Sin is transgressing the commands of God, and there is no one without it:

Romans 3:23   For all have sinned, and come short of the glory of God.

What can we do now that we can no longer conduct ourselves as though our sins have no effect upon society—for we know that is farthest from the truth? God is looking upon each country as one body. America is one body. If we are considered to be one body in the eyes of God when we are judged, I wonder what it is that God sees when he is looking at us. We know that all sins become a part of the problem. If we were to gather all the sin in America and roll it into a ball, I wonder how big that ball has become. Will the righteousness ball outweigh the sin ball? This is an idea of what God sees when he looks upon a body of people. He sees all sin as one; therefore, understanding the mind of God and how he views things is a knowledge that must be made known.

Isaiah 55:8-9   For my thoughts are not your thoughts, neither are your ways my ways, saith the Lord.

For as the heavens are higher than the earth, so are my ways higher than your ways, and my thoughts than your thoughts.

If we will begin to learn the ways of God, it will help us to understand just how much impact our individual ways and actions have on society as a whole. For too long our thoughts have been directed toward ourselves, not realizing that our individual ways and actions have a great influence in the world in which we live. The second greatest command recorded in the law of God is that we are to love our neighbor as ourselves.

Matthew 22:37-40   Jesus said unto him, thou shalt love the Lord thy God with all thy heart, and with all thy soul, and with all thy mind.

This is the first and great commandment.

And the second is like unto it, thou shalt love thy neighbor as thyself.

On these two commandments hang all the law and the prophets.

This commandment is so important because our individual ways and actions have an effect on others. If we truly love each other, we will not do things that would cause trouble to come to others or to our nation. We are all members in the body of America, and whatever we do affects other Americans. When prayer is made for us, sin will determine whether the prayer request is answered. If sin is found to be dominant over righteousness, the prayer request is delayed by the sin and will remain delayed until righteousness rules over sin. And while sin is ruling, destruction is made possible. But when we begin to love each other as ourselves, we will become mindful of the things we do in fear that we can hinder or alter the movement of God not only in our life, but also in the lives of others and our country. Love will cause us to be mindful of these things, fearing that we might be opening the door to the devil, allowing him to bring calamity upon all.

Knowing how God operates will help protect us from the schemes and tricks of the devil. Acts of evil can only take place where seeds of evil were planted. Every seed produces after its own kind. If righteousness is dominant among people and others desire evil of that people in which righteousness is dominant, the righteousness prevents the evil from happening. The outcome always depends upon who is in charge. Righteousness and unrighteousness have nothing in common. They cannot reign in the same place; the strongest will always rule the weakest. This is true whether the situation is in a country, a city, town, state, marriage, or in the family. If unrighteousness is allowed to reign among the people, it opens the door for bad things to happen in their midst. If righteousness is allowed to reign, it becomes both a covering and protection from evil. Weapons may form, but they will not prosper.

Isaiah 54:17   No weapon that is formed against thee shall prosper; and every tongue that shall rise against thee in judgement thou shalt condemn. This is the heritage of the servants of the Lord, and their righteousness is of me, saith the Lord.

I just love the word of God because it will not return to him void, it will accomplish whatever he sends it to do.

Corporate sinning is the most dangerous. It involves more than one person. Because of the involvement of more than one person, this sin should be taken seriously—a multitude of people or a whole city can be involved. I am reminded of two cities in the Bible—Sodom and Gomorrah—that were completely destroyed because of corporate sin. Only God himself knows the consequences people will endure because of corporate sin.

For this reason, God gives a command instead of a law. He knows the severity of the consequences if the command is broken. The most wonderful thing about God is that he wants what is best for us. He proved this to be true when he gave us his best—Jesus Christ—to become a ransom for our sin. Therefore, we can see that God is not mean or demanding, but that he is trying to protect us from the enemy that we just do not know or fully understand. Look at what the enemy did to New Orleans. Who could have imagined such a thing? But God knew that the enemy is capable of doing things like this. This is why he is consistently speaking through his ministers giving warning to his people.

Proverbs 14: 34   Righteousness exalteth a nation: but sin is a reproach to any people.

This maybe is a hard meal to digest for some because we know God as a loving God. Most people wonder how a loving God can allow this to happen. But I want to let you know God is not the destroyer, but he created the destroyer to destroy the wicked. Bad things come from the devil, and sin allows him to work. It is the thing that gives the devil an assignment.

Isaiah 54:16   Behold, I have created the smith that bloweth the coals in the fire, and that bringeth forth an instrument for his work; and I have created the destroyer to destroy.

God created the destroyer, who is the devil, to keep creation from becoming a wicked place. When we sin we move ourselves from the protection and covering of a loving God to a place where the devil rules. In this sinful place, all kinds of bad things are taking place. We do need to understand God and how he operates because we have a choice to make. We need to decide whose side we want to serve on, whether it will be God or the devil. When we talk about being born again, we talk about making a choice to serve the Lord; this is what it means. In doing this, we protect ourselves and help protect our family, community, city, state, and country from acts of evil.

I know some may say, my loved one was born again and a bad thing happened to them. This is the act of corporate sin at work, and innocent people are paying the price for the wicked. Because of the danger of this type of sin, we must remember that whatever sin we commit has an effect on everyone in the region. Whether we like it or not, we are all one. And our individual behavior, whether it is known or unknown, affects everyone. For example, what happened to the twin towers was the act of corporate sin, meaning there were more sinful activities going on in America that day than righteous acts. Because of sin, the enemy was able to form his weapon and execute his evil acts, which he had long planned. The word of God tells us that the weapon may form, but it will not prosper. But this is for those whose righteousness is of God. Every person in those towers was not a sinner, but because sin ruled that day, they got caught in the wrong place at the wrong time. Even those in the airplanes lost their lives because sin was ruling that day. If righteousness was ruling, I do not care what the enemy planned. He would not have been able to execute his plan. He could have formed a weapon, but it would not have come to pass.

Isaiah 54:14 and 17   In righteousness shalt thou be established: thou shalt be far from oppression; for thou shalt not fear: and from terror; for it shall not come near thee.

No weapon that is formed against thee shall prosper; and every tongue that shall rise against thee in judgment thou shalt condemn. This is the heritage of the servants of the Lord, and their righteousness is of me, saith the Lord.

The enemy, which is the devil, can only operate where there is sin. He needs negative energy to be dominant to execute his plans; he cannot operate on positive energy. If we take a look around the world and observe some of the tragedies that we have faced, we can only imagine the kind of negative energy it takes to produce these things. Think about the amount of electrical current it takes to operate a country. Electricity is energy; it can be negative or positive. If we do a study, we can get an idea about how negative and positive energies work in creation. We have seen terminal diseases, hunger, poverty, wars, car bombings, decapitation of human beings, terror, unlawful sexual acts, kidnapping, child molestation, pornography, bad weather, gangs, tsunamis just to name a few, but there are many others. All these calamities that are coming upon creation come because there is more negative energy than positive energy. Sin produces negative energy, and righteousness produces positive energy.

In grade school, we learned that whatever is dominant is what controls. So we know that the root to this problem lies within each of us; therefore, we need to take the necessary measures to eliminate the sin in our individual lives. I believe that when sin diminishes in America, she will again take her rightful place on earth and in the heart of God. The enemy will no longer be able to rule in America. So let us be true to ourselves. If we judge ourselves, we can escape the judgment of God.

1 Corinthians 11:31   For if we would judge ourselves, we should not be judged.

To judge ourselves means to look into our own life through the word of God. If we find an area in our life where we are transgressing the commandments, let us take the necessary measures to correct the problem. Keep in mind that there are laws governing all acts of disobedience. It may seem cruel that God would judge his people, but God is looking to see if we are doing what he commanded us to do concerning the earth. He wants to see if we are worthy to have dominion over the earth, or does he need to create another people to take care of the earth. We must not forget that the commands of God were written over two thousand years ago, long before we were ever born. This is the reason God told Hosea that his people were destroyed for the lack of knowledge. God knew his people would disobey him from the beginning of time. He is the beginning and the end. He knew what his people would be doing in the end—the very moment he blew breath into their nostrils. Because God is the beginning and the end, we can read in the Bible about things happening today that were written over two thousand years ago.

Revelation 22:13   I am Alpha and Omega, the beginning and the end, the first and the last.

We are being destroyed because of what we do not know, not because of what we know. There are a lot of highly educated men and women in America, yet something is missing, and we know this because of all the misfortunes that are happening around us. I am sure if someone knew how to rid our country of terror, gang activity, stealing, killing, and all the other bad things that are happening, they would do it in a heartbeat. But because these things are happening, that lets us know that some knowledge has not been yet revealed.

This is the reason I enquired of the Lord for an answer to this problem. What the Lord said to me are the things I am sharing, that are written in this book. If we would just take the time to judge ourselves by looking into our own life to see what commands we are not keeping. If we would just learn to obey God, we can conquer every situation we face today. Our problem is not the people; our problem is sin. When we allow sin to remain among us, it continues to grow like a newborn infant. It continues to grow until it matures and manifests itself in creation through people. The answer to all of our troubles is found in the word of God, and all sin adds to the problem we share. It is hard to win a battle against crime over others when there is sin in our camp, and Satan cannot cast Satan out.

Matthew 7:3-5   And why beholdest thou the mote that is in thy brother's eye, but considerest not the beam that is in thine own eye? Or how wilt thou say to thy brother, let me pull out the mote out of thine eye; and, behold, a beam is in thine own eye? Thou hypocrite, first cast out the beam out of thine own eye; and then shalt thou see clearly to cast out the mote out of thy brother's eye.

Matthew 12:26   And if Satan cast out Satan, he is divided against himself; how shall then his kingdom stand?

The time has come for us to rid our camp of sin so that we can begin to heal. This process can begin by judging ourselves—and not judging others. To do this, we are going to need to know the truth. These truths that we need, they are found in the word of God. If we learn them, they will set us free.

John 8:31-32   Then said Jesus to those Jews which believed on him, if ye continue in my word, then are ye my disciples indeed;

And ye shall know the truth, and the truth shall make you free.

Recorded in this chapter are some of the commands of God to help us get started. By no means all the commands written in the Bible are recorded in this chapter. These commands are recorded just to help us start on our way to freedom until we can read the Bible in its entirety. Let us try to remember and not forget why keeping the commandments is so important. It is our covering and protection from God. He sent his son Jesus Christ to pay for our redemption with his blood, removing us from under the curse of the law. To be under grace until we come to the fullness of God. When we keep the commandments, we are free from the curse of the law, and nothing can happen to us except it be the will of God. Jehovah God, our Heavenly Father, loved us so much that he would not allow Satan to have lordship over us even after we disobeyed him in the Garden of Eden. Since that time, all power in heaven and in earth have been given to Jesus.

Matthew 28:18   And Jesus came and spake unto them, saying, all power is given unto me in heaven and in earth.

Philippians 2:9-11   Wherefore God also hath highly exalted him, and given him a name which is above every name: That at the name of Jesus every knee should bow, of things in heaven, and things in earth, and things under the earth;

And that every tongue should confess that Jesus Christ is Lord, to the glory of God the Father.

The name of Jesus gives us power over the enemy and gives us access to heaven. Whatever we ask our Heavenly Father in Jesus's name, he will do.

John 14:14   If ye shall ask any thing in my name, I will do it.

To activate this power in our lives, we must first have authority to use Jesus's name. If we have not been given authority to use the name of Jesus, we can ask all we want, and nothing will happen for us. To gain access to the name of Jesus, we must first become born again. This is the process that removes us from being denied to being accepted, from under the law to under grace, until we reach maturity.

Romans 10:9-10   That if thou shalt confess with thy mouth the Lord Jesus, and shall believe in thine heart that God hath raised him from the dead, thou shalt be saved.

For with the heart man believeth unto righteousness; and with the mouth confession is made unto salvation.

After we have become born again, the next step is learning the commandments so that we can obey them. This is a sign that we love the Lord. And if we love the Lord, that means we believe in him.

John 14:12-13   Verily, verily, I say unto you, he that believeth on me, the works that I do shall he do also; and greater works than these shall he do; because I go unto my Father.

And whatsoever ye shall ask in my name, that I will do, that the Father may be glorified in the Son.

Matthew chapter 5 is a chapter I love because I can picture Jesus speaking to America. You are the salt of the earth. America, you are the one chosen to hold everything together. God has shed his grace on you. America he has crowned thy good with brotherhood from sea to shining sea. You are the sweet land of liberty. America land of the noble free. Now, America, if you lose your savor to sin, where with shall you be salted again? You are therefore good for nothing but to be cast out and to be trodden under the feet of men.

This is what Bin Laden knows, and this is why he is trying to execute his plan. So we cannot allow sin to rule in our nation any longer; the stakes are too high, the requirement of God for this country is too great. He created us to be the light of the world, a city that is set upon a hill that cannot be hid. The time has now come for us to return to our God. It is time to let our light shine again among men that they may see our good works and glorify our father, which is in heaven. Come, America, let us return to the word of God—the foundation which we were built upon.

Matthew 7:24-27   Therefore whosoever heareth these sayings of mine, and doeth them, I will liken him unto a wise man, which built his house upon a rock:

And the rain descended, and the floods came, and the winds blew, and beat upon that house; and it fell not: for it was founded upon a rock.

And every one that heareth these sayings of mine, and doeth them not, shall be likened unto a foolish man, which built his house upon the sand:

And the rain descended, and the floods came, and the winds blew, and beat upon that house; and it fell: and great was the fall of it.

Isaiah 1:19-20   If ye be willing and obedient, ye shall eat the good of the land:

                                But if ye refuse and rebel, ye shall be devoured with the sword: for the mouth of the Lord hath spoken it.

In the book of Mathew the fifth chapter, God said whoever shall break the commandments and shall teach others to do so shall be called the least in the kingdom of heaven. But whoever keeps the commandments and teaches others to do so shall be called great in the kingdom of heaven. This is who we are. America, we are considered great in the kingdom of God. But until our righteousness exceeds the righteousness of others, we cannot enter into the blessing of God. God's ways are not our ways, and his thoughts are not our thoughts. What we may think is right may not be right to God. What we think is wrong may not be wrong to God.

Isaiah 55:8-9   For my thoughts are not your thoughts, neither are your ways my ways, saith the Lord

                                For as the heavens are higher than the earth, so are my ways higher than your ways, and my thoughts than your thoughts.

Taking the yoke of God, which is the word of God, and learning his ways is the only way we will master the planet Earth. We are so blessed not for ourselves only, but to be a blessing to others. Therefore, let us not turn our blessing into curses. Let us go back to what our forefathers knew of the word of God and explore the difference between his ways and our ways, between his thoughts and our thoughts. We understand that after we give our life to Christ the next step is to keep the commandments. To do this, we understand that we must know the commandments. Let us begin in the Old Testament law before the coming of Jesus and read some of the commandments given to his servant Moses.

Exodus 20:3-17

- Thou shalt have no other gods before me.
- Thou shalt not make unto thee any graven image, or any likeness of any thing that is in the heaven above, or that is in the earth beneath, or that is in the water under the earth:
- Thou shalt not bow down thyself to them, nor serve them:
- Thou shalt not take the name of the Lord thy God in vain; for the Lord will not hold him guiltless that taketh his name in vain.
- Remember the Sabbath day, to keep it holy.
- Honour thy father and thy mother: that thy days may be long upon the land which the Lord thy God giveth thee.
- Thou shalt not kill.
- Thou shalt not commit adultery.
- Thou shalt not steal.
- Thou shalt not bear false witness against thy neighbour.
- Thy shalt not covet thy neighbour's house, thou shalt not covet thy neighbour's wife, nor his manservant, nor his maidservant, nor his ox, nor his ass, nor any thing that is thy neighbour's.

These commandments can be read in Exodus chapter 20. They were given to Moses for the children of Israel at the time of their departure from bondage out of the land of Egypt. But they are not all the commands that were given at that time. After Israel was freed, God continued to give commandments unto them. You will find these laws recorded in Leviticus chapter 18 and 19. These laws and commandments were given to Moses by God to give to the people; they were guidelines showing the people how to worship, serve, and obey a holy god.

UNLAWFUL SEXUAL RELATIONS

Leviticus 18:6-30

- No one is to approach any close relative to have sexual relations.
- Do not dishonor your father by having sexual relations with your mother.
- Do not have sexual relations with your sister, either your father's daughter or your mother's daughter, whether she was born in the same home or elsewhere. Do not have sexual relations with your son's daughter or your daughter's daughter.
- Do not have sexual relations with the daughter of your father's wife, born to your father; she is your sister.
- Do not have sexual relations with your father's sister; she is your father's close relative.
- Do not have sexual relations with your mother's close relative.
- Do not dishonor your father's brother by approaching his wife to have sexual relations; she is your aunt.
- Do not have sexual relations with your daughter-in-law. She is your son's wife; do not have relations with her.
- Do not have sexual relations with your brother's wife.
- Do not have sexual relations with both a woman and her daughter. Do not have sexual relations with either her son's daughter or her daughter's daughter; they are close relatives. That is wickedness.
- Do not take your wife's sister as a rival wife and have sexual relations with her while your wife is living.
- Do not approach a woman to have sexual relations during the uncleanness of her monthly period.
- Do not have sexual relations with your neighbor's wife and defile yourself with her.
- Do not give any of your children to be sacrificed to Molech, for you must not profane the name of your God. I am the Lord.
- Do not lie with a man as one lies with a woman; that is detestable.

- Do not have sexual relations with an animal and defile yourself with it. A woman must not present herself to an animal to have sexual relations with it; that is a perversion.
- Do not defile yourselves in any of these ways, because this is how the nations that I am going to drive out before you became defiled. Even the land was defiled; so I punished it for its sin, and the land vomited out its inhabitants.

MORAL AND CEREMONIAL LAWS

Leviticus 19:2-37

- Be holy because I, the Lord your God is holy.
- Each of you must respect his mother and father, and observe my Sabbaths.
- Do not turn to idols or make gods of cast metal for yourselves.
- When you sacrifice a fellowship offering to the Lord, sacrifice it in such a way that it will be accepted on your behalf. It shall be eaten on the day you sacrifice it or on the next day; anything left over until the third day must be burned up. If any of it is eaten on the third day, it is impure and will not be accepted. Whoever eats it will be held responsible because he has desecrated what is holy to the Lord; that person must be cut off from his people.
- When you reap the harvest of your land, do not reap to the very edges of your field or gather the gleanings of your harvest. Do not go over your vineyard a second time or pick up the grapes that have fallen. Leave them for the poor and the alien. I am the Lord your God.
- Do not steal.
- Do not lie.
- Do not deceive one another.
- Do not swear falsely by my name and so profane the name of your God. I am the Lord.

- Do not defraud your neighbor or rob him.
- Do not hold back the wages of a hired man overnight.
- Do not curse the deaf or put a stumbling block in front of the blind, but fear God. I am the Lord.
- Do not pervert justice; do not show partiality to the poor or favoritism to the great, but judge your neighbor fairly.
- Do not go about spreading slander among your people.
- Do not do anything that endangers your neighbor's life. I am the Lord.
- Do not hate your brother in your heart. Rebuke your neighbor frankly so you will not share in his guilt.
- Do not seek revenge or bear a grudge against one of your people, but love your neighbor as yourself. I am the Lord.
- Keep my decrees.
- Do not mate different kinds of animals.
- Do not plant your field with two kinds of seed.
- Do not wear clothing woven of two kinds of material.
- If a man sleeps with a woman who is a slave girl promised to another man but who has not been ransomed or given her freedom, there must be due punishment. Yet they are not to be put to death, because she had not been freed. The man, however, must bring a ram to the entrance to the tent of meeting for a guilt offering to the Lord.
- When you enter the land and plant any kind of fruit tree, regard its fruit as forbidden. For three years you are to consider it forbidden; it must not be eaten. In the fourth year all its fruit will be holy, an offering of praise to the Lord. But in the fifth year you may eat its fruit. In this way your harvest will be increased. I am the Lord your God.
- Do not eat any meat with the blood still in it.
- Do not practice divination or sorcery.
- Do not cut the hair at the sides of your head or clip off the edges of your beard.
- Do not cut your bodies for the dead or put tattoo marks on yourselves. I am the Lord.

- Do not degrade your daughter by making her a prostitute, or the land will turn to prostitution and be filled with wickedness.
- Observe my Sabbaths and have reverence for my sanctuary. I am the Lord.
- Do not turn to mediums or seek out spiritists, for you will be defiled by them. I am the Lord your God.
- Rise in the presence of the aged, show respect for the elderly and revere your God. I am the Lord.
- When an alien lives with you in your land, do not mistreat him. The alien living with you must be treated as one of your native-born. Love him as yourself, for you were aliens in Egypt. I am the Lord your God.
- Do not use dishonest standards when measuring length, weight or quantity. Use honest scales and honest weights, an honest ephah and an honest hin. I am the Lord your god, who brought you out of Egypt.
- Keep all my decrees and all my laws and follow them. I am the Lord.

As we read through the laws and commands of God, we can notice that a lot of the commandments are being broken by us. We know this to be truth even by watching the talk shows. I thank God for the talk shows because they are ways of revealing the secret things that are happening in our country. I thank God for all the wonderful people who appear on the talk shows because they let us know what is going on in the secret closets of America.

But my request is, what are we going to do about these behaviors that are being revealed. We know that they are transgressing the commands of God. What steps should be taken now that we know? Should these people be sent away in the manner that they came, or should they receive the help they need to turn their lives around? If this was done, I believe this would be very pleasing in the eyes of God. The Jerry Springer Show by opinion may be the worst talk show on TV, but in the eyes of God, it may be the best for the simple reason that he is dealing with people who need the most help. I believe that it would be nothing short of a miracle for the people who appear on Mr. Springer's show to have a transformation in their lives by receiving the help they need to do so. There is a lot of sinning in America, and I believe a tool that God is using to reveal sin is the talk shows.

Luke 12:2   For there is nothing covered, that shall not be revealed; neither hid, that shall not be known.

What is being done about the sin that has been revealed? Sin is the root of terror, and all sin adds to the problem. It opens the door to the devil; and the devil comes to steal, kill, and destroy. Life is about making a difference in the lives of others, and I do believe we need to recognize the opportunity.

The sermon that Jesus Christ preached on the mount was about having beatitude. A beatitude means speaking to your attitude and telling it to be and it is so. Your attitude becomes what you tell it to become. And after Jesus had preached on attitude, he told his disciples that he had not come to abolish the laws or the prophets, instead he had come to fulfill them.

Matthew 5:17-18   Think not that I am come to destroy the law, or the prophets: I am not come to destroy, but to fulfill.

For verily I say unto you, Till heaven and earth pass, one jot or one tittle shall in no wise pass from the law, till all is fulfilled.

The law given under Moses's ministry was given to the fleshly part of man. It did not minister to the spirit of man. But we know that man is body, spirit, and soul; and we understand that which is flesh comes first, then that which is spirit. The spirit cannot come before the flesh, and when flesh appears, it brings a spirit with it that has the ability to do good and evil. Therefore, man must first become born again and then become educated in the things of the spirit and the flesh. If the spirit of man is not educated and the mind of man is educated or vice versa, you will be an unbalanced person or someone who is unstable. Jesus Christ brought the fulfillment of the commandment by speaking to the spirit of man.

Matthew 5:21 to 7:27

- Ye have heard that it was said by them of old time, thou shalt not kill; and whosoever shall kill shall be in danger of the judgement. But I say unto you, that whosoever is angry with his brother without a cause shall be in danger of the judgement: and whosoever shall say to his brother, Raca, shall be in danger of the council: but whosoever shall say, thou fool, shall be in danger of hell fire.
- Ye have heard that it was said by them of old time, thou shalt not commit adultery. But I say unto you, that whosoever looketh on a woman to lust after her hath committed adultery with her already in his heart.
- It has been said, whosoever shall put away his wife, let him give her a writing of divorcement. But I say unto you, that whosoever shall put away his wife, saving for the cause of fornication, causeth her to commit adultery. And whosoever shall marry her that is divorced committeth adultery.
- Ye have heard that it hath been said by them of old time, Thou shalt not forswear thyself, but shalt perform unto the Lord thine oaths. But I say unto you, swear not at all; neither by heaven; for it is God's throne: nor by earth; for it is his footstool: neither by Jerusalem; for it is the city of the great king. Neither shalt thou swear by thy head, because thou canst not make one hair white or black. But let your communication be yea, yea; nay, nay: for whatsoever is more than these cometh of evil.
- You have heard that it hath been said, an eye for an eye, and a tooth for a tooth: but I say unto you, that ye resist not evil: but whosoever shall smite thee on thy right cheek, turn to him the other also. And if any man will sue thee at the law, and take away thy coat, let him have thy cloke also. And whosoever shall compel thee to go a mile, go with him two. Give to him that asketh thee, and from him that would borrow of thee turn not thou away.

- Ye have heard that it hath been said, thou shalt love thy neighbor, and hate thine enemy. But I say unto you, love your enemies, bless them that curse you, do good to the them that hate you, and pray for them which despitefully use you, and persecute you; That ye may be the children of your father which is in heaven: for he maketh his sun to rise on the evil and on the good, and sendeth rain on the just and on the unjust. For if ye love them which love you, what reward have ye? Do not even the publicans the same? And if you salute your brethren only, what do you more than others? Do not even the publicans so? Be you therefore perfect, even as your father which is in heaven is perfect.

- Take heed that ye do not your alms before men, to be seen of them: otherwise ye have no reward of your father which is in heaven.

- When thou prayest, thou shalt not be as the hypocrites are: for they love to pray standing in the synagogues and in the corners of the streets, that they may be seen of men. Verily I say unto you, they have their reward.

- But thou, when thou prayest, enter into thy closet, and when thou hast shut thy door, pray to thy father which is in secret; and thy father which seeth in secret shall reward thee openly.

- But when ye pray, use not vain repetitions, as the heathen do: for they think that they shall be heard for their much speaking.

- After this manner therefore pray ye: Our father which art in heaven, hallowed be thy name. Thy kingdom come. Thy will be done in earth, as it is in heaven. Give us this day our daily bread. And forgive us our debts, as we forgive our debtors. And lead us not into temptation, but deliver us from evil. For thine is the kingdom, and the power, and the glory, forever. Amen.

- Moreover when ye fast, be not, as the hypocrites, of a sad countenance: for they disfigure their faces that they may appear unto men to fast. Verily I say unto you, they have their reward.

- But thou, when thou fastest, anoint thine head, and wash thy face; that thou appear not unto men to fast, but unto thy father which is in secret: and thy father, which seeth in secret, shall reward thee openly.

- Lay not up for yourselves treasures upon earth, where moth and rust doth corrupt, and where thieves break through and steal. But lay up for yourselves treasure in heaven, where neither moth nor rust doth corrupt, and where thieves do not break through nor steal. For where your treasure is, there will your heart be also.

- No man can serve two masters: for either he will hate the one, and love the other; or else he will hold to the one, and despise the other. You cannot serve God and mammon.

- Therefore take no thought for your life, what ye shall eat, or what ye shall drink; nor yet for your body, what ye shall put on. Is not the life more than meat, and the body than raiment?

- But seek ye first the kingdom of God, and his righteousness; and all these things shall be added unto you.

- Take therefore no thought for the morrow: for the morrow shall take thought for the things of itself. Sufficient unto the day is the evil thereof.

- Judge not, that ye be not judged

- Give not that which is holy unto the dogs, neither cast ye your pearls before swine, lest they trample them under their feet, and turn again and rend you.

- Ask, and it shall be given you; seek, and ye shall find; knock, and it shall be opened unto you.

- Therefore all things whatsoever ye would that men should do to you, do ye even so to them: for this is the law and the prophets.

- Enter ye in at the strait gate (which is Jesus Christ): for wide is the gate, and broad is the way, that leadeth to destruction, and many there be which go in thereat. Because strait is the gate, and narrow is the way, which leadeth unto life, and few there be that find it.

- Beware of false prophets, which come to you in sheep's clothing, but inwardly they are ravening wolves. Ye shall know them by their fruits. Do men gather grapes of thorns, or figs of thistles?

- Not every one that saith unto me, Lord, Lord, shall enter into the kingdom of heaven; but he that doeth the will of my father, which is in heaven.

- Therefore whosoever heareth these sayings of mine, and doeth them, I will liken him unto a wise man, which built his house upon a rock. And the rain descended, and the floods came, and the winds blew, and beat upon that house; and it fell not: for it was founded upon a rock. And everyone that heareth these sayings of mine, and doeth them not, shall be likened unto a foolish man, which built his house upon the sand. And the rain descended, and the floods came, and the winds blew, and beat upon that house; and it fell: and great was the fall of it.

As we read though the commandments, we can easily find areas where we are in disobedience. I love the word of God because it tells me that we cannot condemn or judge each other, but we have a responsibility for correcting ourselves.

John 3:17   For God sent not his Son into the world to condemn the world; but that the world through him might be saved.

Understanding that we cannot judge or condemn each other leaves only one thing to be done—that is to judge ourselves. Everyone is guilty of something. There is no one without sin.

Romans 3:23   For all have sinned, and come short of the glory of God.

1 John 1:8-10   If we say that we have no sin, we deceive ourselves, and the truth is not in us.

                 If we confess our sins, he is faithful and just to forgive us our sins, and to cleanse us from all unrighteousness.

                 If we say that we have not sinned, we make him a liar, and his word is not in us.

Having the information and the understanding that we need, we can make an effort in keeping the commandments. The importance of our task gives us the courage to move forward and build a better world for our children, our grandchildren, and for ourselves. We have the power, which is the power of choice, and it is up to each one of us to make the right decision. Researching the commandments and locating the areas where we are falling short is one sure way that we can help our country. After finding these areas of shortcoming, let us confess our sins to God, and he will forgive us and cleanse us from all unrighteousness.

1 John 1:9   If we confess our sins, he is faithful and just to forgive us our sins, and to cleanse us from all unrighteousness.

Now that we know the truth, we are without excuse if we continue in sin; and if we do continue in sin, it is because we have made a choice to do so. If we have made a choice to continue sinning, we will surely pay the price for it that is written in the word of God.

Galatians 6:7   Be not deceived; God is not mocked: for whatsoever a man soweth, that shall he also reap.

In the eyes of God, we are one body, one nation, and everyone's sin adds to the problems which we are experiencing in America. There is only one question left to be asked of us at this time; that is, are your sins killing America? After we have read through the Old and New Testament laws and have been found guilty of breaking the commandments, the answer to the question is yes, our sin is helping to kill America. We know what sin is doing to our world, so what are we going to do about it? Are we going to continue on in sin until we completely destroy our country? Or will we turn, repent for our sins, and save our world?

This is a matter of the heart, and repentance takes place on the individual level. We cannot repent for each other, and if we choose to overlook the truth, how can we address the terrible things that happen to us, which come because of sin? Continual sinning will cause a continual sin reaction.

Romans 6:23   For the wages of sin is death; but the gift of God is eternal life through Jesus Christ (the word made flesh) our Lord.

If someone is wondering what do his or her sin has to do with the country, the answer is nothing—if you do not live in the country. But if you live in America, your sins add to the problems in America simply because you are a member of the country. In the eyes of God, we are considered one body among the many countries, which have many members. This requires every man, woman, boy, and girl of age to be responsible for eliminating the sin in their life through repentance.

When God created man, he used the same plan he used when he created the earth. If you want to know how the world is supposed to operate, study your own body. Our natural body is one body with many members. We have a head, neck, limbs, chest, abdominals, back, buttocks. We have the organs, five senses, tissues, cells, muscles, bones, and so on until all the members of the natural body are named. God created each member of our natural body to perform a particular duty. So likewise, every person is created to perform a particular duty within a country. God has created each country to fulfill a certain duty on the earth.

The question for each country is, are you fulfilling the duties that God created you to do? We have to continue to remind ourselves that God does not create anything without a purpose. Everything and every being in creation has a purpose. I wonder how many people in the world know the purpose God has for their life. I wonder when we return home to the father what our reward will be. Will it be, "Well done, my good and faithful servant, enter to rest." Or will it be, "Depart from me, you worker of iniquity."

These are just a few thoughts written to capture our attention and keep us focused on doing what is right. There is only one thing that will hinder a person or a country from fulfilling their purpose in the earth—that is sin. Sin separates and love binds together. As the members in the natural body are connected and work together, so likewise the members of the country need to be connected and to work together. As members in the natural body need each other, so do the members in the country need each other.

1 Corinthians 12:14-26   For the body is not one member, but many.

If the foot shall say, because I am not the hand, I am not of the body; is it therefore not of the body?

And if the ear shall say, because I am not the eye, I am not of the body; is it therefore not of the body?

If the whole body were an eye, where were the hearing? If the whole were hearing, where were the smelling?

But now hath God set the members every one of them in the body, as it hath pleased him.

And if they were all one member, where were the body?

But now are they many members, yet but one body.

And the eye cannot say unto the hand, I have no need of thee: nor again the head to the feet, I have no need of you.

Nay, much more those members of the body, which seem to be more feeble, are necessary:

And those members of the body, which we think to be less honorable, upon these we bestow more abundant honor; and our uncomely parts have more abundant comeliness.

For our comely parts have no need: but God hath tempered the body together, having given more abundant honor to that part which lacked:

That there should be no schism in the body; but that the members should have the same care one for another.

And whether one member suffers, all the members suffer with it; or one member be honored, all the members rejoice with it.

Every member that God has placed in the body has a purpose and is needed. To make the world go round, we are responsible for not only becoming a healthy body, but also for teaching others how to become healthy. America can no longer take things for granted; we cannot do as others do. We are chosen to be a leader in the world by God. He could have chosen any country, but he chose America. And instead of teaching others righteousness, we have allowed others to teach us unrighteousness. This is a trick of the enemy that must be stopped at once. We must take control of our country and its responsibilities again.

Matthew 5:19   Whosoever therefore shall break one of these least commandments, and shall teach men so, he shall be called the least in the kingdom of heaven: but whosoever shall do and teach them, the same shall be called great in the kingdom of heaven.

America was once looked upon as being great because she had the ability to make others great. But now she has lost her greatness to sin, and she is no longer looked upon as a great nation. Sin weakens, it causes the loss of strength, and it takes away the glow that reveals the beauty within. Because of sin, where America was once able to prevent war, now she is inducing war.

America, what is happening to you? I remember when your word was your bond, but now no one believes in you; your own people are losing faith in you. Is sin worth this shame that has come upon you? Is it asking too much for us to accept what God is doing to us? We are all connected, and what affects one affects all. Look at it this way, America, when illness enters the natural body the sickness affects the whole body. So likewise within the country, the sin affects the whole.

Matthew 22:39   Thou shalt love thy neighbor as thyself.

Seeing that a country works somewhat like the natural body should motivate us to unite like never before; after all, this is the United States of America. If there is a terminal illness in the human body, unless it is removed or destroyed, it will destroy the body. In the body of the country, there are certain sins that work as terminal illnesses. Prejudice, racism, hatred, envy, jealousy, all forms of unnatural sexual activity just to name a few, these will cause a terminal illness.

Another way to understand terminal illness in the body of the country is to see it as anything that will cause the members to disconnect. When this happens, the body becomes weak, feeble, and can no longer perform the duties it was created to do. Whenever there is a disconnecting of the body within a country, you will observe a lot of destruction taking place, which is what we are seeing in America today. Instead of waging a good warfare and being successful at helping others, the members have begun to fight among themselves. Like cancer in the natural body, it is not satisfied until is has destroyed the whole body.

Galatians 5:13-26

For, brethren, ye have been called unto liberty; only use not liberty for an occasion to the flesh, but by love serve one another.

For all the law is fulfilled in one word, even in this; thou shall love thy neighbor as thyself.

But if ye bite and devour one another, take heed that ye are not consumed one of another.

This I say then, walk in the Spirit (word of God), and ye shall not fulfil the lust of the flesh (which is sin).

For the flesh lusteth against the Spirit, and the Spirit against the flesh: and these are contrary the one to the other: so that ye cannot do the things that you would.

But if ye were led of the Spirit, ye are not under the law.

Now the works of the flesh are manifest, which are these; adultery, fornication, uncleanness, and lasciviousness:

Idolatry, witchcraft, hatred, variance, emulations, wrath, strife, seditions, heresies,

Envying, murders, drunkenness, revellings, and such like: of the which I tell you before, as I have also told you in time past, that they which do such things shall not inherit the kingdom of God.

But the fruit of the Spirit is love, joy, peace, longsuffering, gentleness, goodness, faith:

Meekness, temperance: against such there is no law.

And they that are Christ's have crucified the flesh with the affections and lusts.

If we live in the Spirit, let us also walk in the Spirit.

Let us not be desirous of vainglory, provoking one another, envying one another.

There is no time for fighting in America; she can no longer be cast out. She must gird herself and take her rightful place on earth. It is time for America to become who God created her to be. She can and she will fulfill the great commission from God. Jesus is soon to come, and he said when he comes we must be found working.

Matthew 24:45-46   Who then is a faithful and wise servant, whom his Lord hath made ruler over his household, to give them meat in due season?

Blessed is that servant, whom his Lord when he cometh shall find so doing.

CHAPTER EIGHT

BEING CONNECTED

I believe we have come to a place in our hearts and minds where we as a people understand the importance of being connected. Being connected will bring many advantages that will allow many great accomplishments. One advantage that being connected brings to the table is strength. Strength will allow one to be powerful physically, intellectually, and morally. With these attributes, there is nothing that America cannot do. She is one nation, one country, a body of members that has obtain physical, intellectual, and moral power through unification. Because America has now become a body of members working together, peace, love, joy, and harmony can be seen coming from her, around the world. She has heard the word of God because she has obeyed the word of God, and now she is victorious in whatever she sets her hands and mind to do. Unity is such a powerful thing. Because of unity, the oneness of the people, in the book of Genesis they were able to build a tower that would have reached heaven, except that God confused the language—America has become this people.

Genesis 11:1-8   And the whole earth was of one language, and of one speech.

And it came to pass, as they journeyed from the east, that they found a plain in the land of Shinar; and they dwelt there.

And they said one to another, Go to, let us build us a city and a tower, whose top may reach unto heaven; and let us make us a name, lest we be scattered abroad upon the face of the whole earth.

And the Lord came down to see the city and the tower, which the children of men builded.

And the Lord said, behold, the people is one, and they have all one language; and this they begin to do: and nothing will be restrained from them, which they have imagined to do.

Go to, let us go down, and there confound their language, that they may not understand one another's speech.

So the Lord scattered them abroad from thence upon the face of all the earth: and they left off to build the city.

Because of unity, being connected and in one accord, in the book of Acts a group of people in an upper room was filled with the spirit of God. The presence of God that filled the lives of everyone in that room that day allowed them to do things no ordinary people could do—America has become this people.

Acts 2:1-4   And when the day of Pentecost was fully come, they were all with one accord in one place. And suddenly there came a sound from heaven as of a rushing mighty wind, and it filled all the house where they were sitting.

And they appeared unto them cloven tongues like as of fire, and it sat upon each of them.

> And they were all filled with the Holy Ghost, and began to speak with other tongues, as the Spirit gave them utterance.

Advantage upon advantage has been given to America because of her oneness and obedience to the commands of God. Being in one accord, Americans work well together. They care for each other, and they have no desire to hurt each other. Their behavior has made keeping the commandments easier because of the manifestation of love that is revealed in America. A source of love is pouring out of America that has never been seen on earth before. People of every tongue and from every nation desire to come and see the light that is shining in America and to feel the love she gives. Because she has perfected her love by loving herself, she has no fears. America has come to know that of all the advantages that being connected has to offer, love is the most powerful; it covers a multitude of sins, and we Americans have it.

1Peter 4:8   And above all things have fervent charity among yourselves: for charity shall cover the multitude of sins.

Romans 13:10   Love worketh no ill to his neighbor: therefore love is the fulfilling of the law.

God is love, and he dwells in America because she has love one for another. America has become a happy nation, and God is pleased with her. She has gained respect from other nations, and once again, she is being called great because of the love she now has. Love always looks for ways to help those who are in need. America has become so strong until she strengthened and delivered her members from sin without condemnation and without judgment but with love. Once again, America has awakened to the truth. And the Holy Bible has become her guide, for she now knows the truth, and the truth has made her free.

Romans 3:4   God forbid: yea let God be true, but every man a liar:
as it is written, that thou mightest be justified in thy
sayings, and mightest overcome when thou art judged.

John 8:31-32   Then said Jesus to those Jews which believed on him, If ye
continue in my word, then are ye my disciples indeed;

And ye shall know the truth, and the truth shall make
you free.

Freedom is found in the continuing obedience to the word of God. Unless it is written in the word of God, it may be a fact, but it may not be the truth. America is no longer sleeping; she has risen and has taken off corruption and has put on incorruption. She has removed mortality and has put on immortality, and now she has the victory over sin, over the terrorist her enemy—the devil.

1 Corinthians 15:51   Behold, I shew you a mystery; We shall not all sleep, but
we shall all be changed,

In a moment, in the twinkling of an eye, at the last
trump: for the trumpet shall sound, and the dead shall
be raised incorruptible, and we shall be changed.

For this corruption must put on incorruption, and
this mortal shall have put on immortality, then shall
be brought to pass the saying that is written, Death is
swallowed up in victory.

O death, where is thy sting? o grave, where is thy victory?

The sting of death is sin; and the strength of sin is the law.

But thanks be to God, which giveth us the victory through our lord Jesus Christ.

The pledge of allegiance tells us that America is one nation under God, not many nations. Therefore, America puts no other God before her God. She knows that where there is more than one God, trouble will arrive because of the difference in opinions. She knows when these things happen, they cause the people to become disconnected, and the Bible tells us that a house divided will not stand.

Mark 3:24-26   And if a kingdom be divided against itself, that kingdom cannot stand.

And if a house be divided against itself, that house cannot stand.

And if Satan rise up against himself, and be divided, he cannot stand, but hath an end.

America has once again become visible among the nations; her light can once again be seen by others. Because of her obedience to God, she has become a city on the hill that cannot be hid. She has become the candlestick that is giving light to all in the world. She is the salt of the earth that has not lost it savor.

Matthew 5:13-16   Ye are the salt of the earth: but if the salt have lost his savour, wherewith shall it be salted? It is thenceforth good for nothing, but to be cast out, and to be trodden under foot of men.

Ye are the light of the world. A city that is set on an hill cannot be hid.

Neither do men light a candle, and put it under a bushel, but on a candlestick; and it giveth light unto all that are in the house.

Let your light so shine (America) before men, that they may see your good works, and glorify your Father which is in heaven.

America is a nation of liberty. She has opened her doors to many nations. To nations that do not understand her God. The God of America is a God of liberty, freedom, and justice for all mankind. But he tells her not to use freedom as an occasion to commit sin, but instead to use her freedom to free others.

Galatians 5:13   For, brethren, ye have been called unto liberty; only use not liberty for an occasion to the flesh, but by love serve one another.

America is a country of justice for all. Our God is greatly to be feared in our country and to be held in reverence by all those around him. His faithfulness surrounds him; his righteousness and justice are the foundation of his throne. He tells America that she must live by his words because she is the apple of his eye, the sheep of his pasture; therefore, she must not go astray.

Exodus 20:3   Thou shalt have no other gods before me.

Psalm 89:7-8, 14, and 18   God is greatly to be feared in the assembly of the saints, and to be had in reverence of all them that are about him.

O Lord God of hosts, who is a strong Lord like unto thee? Or to thy faithfulness round about thee?

Justice and judgment are the habitation of thy throne: mercy and truth shall go before thy face.

For the Lord is our defence; and the Holy One of Israel is our king.

Psalm 100:3

Know ye that the Lord he is God: it is he that hath made (America) us, and not we ourselves; we are his people, and the sheep of his pasture.

Galatians 3:11

But that no man is justified by the law in the sight of God, it is evident: for, The just shall live by faith.

Revelation 22:18-19

For I testify unto every man that heareth the words of the prophecy of this book, If any man shall add unto these things, God shall add unto him the plagues that are written in this book:

And if any man shall take away from the words of the book of this prophecy, God shall take away his part out of the book of life, and out of the holy city and from the things which are written in this book.

Matthew 21:43

Therefore say I unto you, The kingdom of God shall be taken from you, and given to a nation bringing forth the fruits thereof.

Matthew 5:18

For verily I say unto you, Till heaven and earth pass, one jot or one tittle shall in no wise pass from the law, till all be fulfilled.

Luke 16:17   And it is easier for heaven and earth to pass, than one tittle of the law to fail.

John 1:1   In the beginning was the Word, and the Word was with God, and the Word was God.

Being connected is the only way a nation can live victorious lives. When choices to live outside of the word of God are embraced, heartache and pain are experienced, and there will always be trouble, calamity, and all sorts of bad things taking place. But the people have the power that has been given to us by God. Our power is the choice we have been given—the right to make decisions how we want to live our lives. The people have the right to live by the word of God, or they can choose not to live by the word of God. Whatever choice is made, remember that there are already written consequences in the word of God judging each choice. When choosing to live by God's word, the people will be blessed. Thank God for your choice. America, you have chosen to obey God, and now you shall live, you are blessed.

Deuteronomy 28:1-14   Now it shall come to pass, if thou shalt hearken diligently to the voice of the Lord thy God, to observe and to do all his commandments which I command thee this day, that the Lord thy God will set thee on high above all nations of the earth.

And all these blessings shall come on thee and overtake thee, if thou shalt hearken unto the voice of the Lord thy God:

Blessed shalt thou be in the city, and blessed shalt thou be in the field.

Blessed shall be the fruit of thy body, and the fruit of thy ground, and the fruit of thy cattle, the increase of thy kine and the flocks of thy sheep.

Blessed shall be thy basket and thy store.

Blessed shalt thou be when thou comest in, and blessed shalt thou be when thou goest out.

The Lord shall cause thine enemies that rise up against thee to be smitten before thy face; they shall come out against thee one way, and flee before thee seven ways.

The Lord shall command the blessing upon thee in thy storehouses, and in all that thou settest thine hand unto; and he shall bless thee in the land which the Lord thy God giveth thee.

The Lord shall establish thee a holy people unto himself, as he has sworn to thee, if thou shalt keep the commandments of the Lord thy God and walk in his ways.

And all people of the earth shall see that thou art called by the name of the Lord; and they shall be afraid of thee.

And the Lord shall make thee plenteous in goods, in the fruit of thy body, and in the fruit of thy cattle, and in the fruit of thy ground, in the land which the Lord sware unto thy fathers to give to thee.

The Lord shall open unto thee his good treasure, the heaven to give the rain unto thy land in his season, and to bless all the work of thine hand: and thou shalt lend unto many nations, and thou shalt not borrow.

And the Lord shall make thee the head and not the tail; and thou shalt be above only, and thou shalt not be beneath; if that thou hearken unto the commandments of the Lord thy God, which I command thee this day, to observe and to do them;

And thou shalt not go aside from any of the words which I command thee this day, to the right hand, or to the left, to go after other gods to serve them.

For all of those whose choice is not to obey God, not to live by his commandments, this is for you:

Deuteronomy 28:15-68   But it shall come to pass, if thou wilt not hearken unto the voice of the Lord thy God, to observe to do all his commandments and his statutes which I command thee this day; that all these curses shall come upon thee and overtake thee:

Cursed shalt thou be in the city, and cursed shalt thou be in the field.

Cursed shall be thy basket and thy store.

Cursed shall be the fruit of thy body, and the fruit of thy land, the increase of thy kine, and the flocks of y sheep.

Cursed shalt thou be when thou comest in, and cursed shalt thou be when thou goest out.

The Lord shall send upon thee cursing, vexation, and rebuke in all that thou settest thine hand unto for to do, until thou be destroyed, and until thou perish quickly; because of the wickedness of thy doings, whereby thou hast forsaken me.

The Lord shall make the pestilence cleave unto thee, until he hath consumed thee from off the land, wither thou goest to possess it.

The Lord shall smite thee with consumption, and with a fever, and with an inflammation, and with an extreme burning, and with the sword, and with blasting, and with mildew; and they shall pursue thee until thou perish.

And thy heaven that is over thy head shall be brass, and the earth that is under thee shall be iron.

The Lord shall make the rain of thy land powder and dust; from heaven shall it come down upon thee until thou be destroyed.

The Lord shall cause thee to be smitten before thine enemies; thou shalt go out one way against them, and flee seven ways before them: and shalt be removed into all the kingdoms of the earth.

And thy carcase shall be meat unto all fowls of the air, and unto the beasts of the earth, and no man shall fray them away.

The Lord will smite thee with the botch of Egypt, and with the emerods, and with the scab, and with the itch; whereof thou canst not be healed.

The Lord shall smite thee with madness, and blindness, and astonishment of heart:

And thou shalt grope at noonday, as the blind gropeth in darkness, and thou shalt not prosper in thy ways: and thou shalt be only oppressed and spoiled evermore, and no man shall save thee.

Thou shalt betroth a wife, and another man shall lie with her; thou shalt build an house, and thou shalt not dwell therein: thou shalt plant a vineyard, and shalt not gather the grapes thereof.

Thine ox shall be slain before thine eyes, and thou shalt not eat thereof: thine ass shall be violently taken away before thy face, and shall not be restored to thee: thy sheep shall be given unto thine enemies, and thou shalt have none to rescue them.

Thy sons and thy daughters shall be given unto another people, and your thine eyes shall look, and fall with longing for them all the day long; and there shall be no might in thine hand.

The fruit of thy land, and all thy labours, shall a nation which thou knowest not eat up; and thou shalt be only oppressed and crushed alway:

So that thou shalt be mad for the sight of thine eyes which thou shalt see.

The Lord shall smite thee in the knees, and in the legs, with a sore botch that cannot be healed, from the sole of thy foot unto the top of thy head.

The Lord shall bring thee, and thy king which thou shalt set over thee, unto a nation which neither thou nor thy fathers have known; and there shalt thou serve other gods, wood and stone.

And thou shalt become an astonishment, a proverb, and a byword, among all nations whither the Lord shall lead thee.

Thou shalt carry much seed out into the field and shalt gather but little in; for the locust shall consume it.

Thou shalt plant vineyards, and dress them, but shalt neither drink of the wine, nor gather the grapes; for the worms shall eat them.

Thou shalt have olive trees throughout all thy coasts, but thou shalt not anoint thyself with the oil; for thine olive shall cast his fruit

Thou shalt beget sons and daughters, but thou shalt not be enjoy them; for they shall go into captivity.

All thy trees and fruit of thy land shall the locust consume.

The stranger that is within thee shall get up above thee very high; and thou shalt come down very low.

He shall lend to thee, and thou shalt not lend to him: he shall be the head, and thou shalt be the tail.

Moreover all these curses shall come upon thee, and shall pursue thee, and overtake thee, til thou be destroyed; because thou hearkenedst not unto the voice of the Lord thy God, to keep his commandments and his statutes which he commanded thee:

And they shall be upon thee for a sign and for a wonder, and upon thy seed for ever.

Because thou servedst not the Lord thy God with joyfulness, and with gladness of heart, for the abundance of all things;

Therefore shalt thou serve thine enemies which the Lord shall send against thee, in hunger, and in thirst, and in nakedness, and in want of all things: and he shall put a yoke of iron upon thy neck until he have destroyed thee.

The Lord shall bring a nation against thee from far, from the end of the earth, as swift as the eagle flieth, a nation whose tongue thou shalt not understand;

A nation of fierce countenance, which shall not regard the person of the old, nor shew favor to the young:

And he shall eat the fruit of thy cattle, and the fruit of thy land, until thou be destroyed: which also shall not leave thee either corn, wine, or oil, or the fruit of thy kine, or thy flocks of sheep, until he have destroyed thee.

And he shall besiege thee in all thy gates, until thy high and fenced walls come down, wherein thou trustedth, throughout all thy land: and he shall besiege thee in all thy gates throughout all thy land, which the Lord thy God hath given thee.

And thou shalt eat the fruit of thine own body, the flesh of thy sons and of thy daughters, which the Lord thy God has given thee, in the siege, and in the straitness, wherewith thine enemies shall distress thee:

So that the man that is tender among you, and very delicate, his eye shall be evil toward his brother, and toward the wife of his bosom, and toward the remnant of his children which he shall leave:

So that he will not give to any of them the flesh of his children whom he shall eat: because he has nothing left him in the siege, and in the straitness, wherewith thine enemies shall distress thee in all thy gates.

The tender and delicate woman among you, which would not adventure to set the sole of her foot upon the ground for delicateness and tenderness, her eye shall be evil toward the husband of her bosom, and toward her son, and toward her daughter,

And toward her young one that cometh out from between her feet, and toward her children which she shall bear: for she shall eat them for want of all things secretly in the siege and straitness, wherein thine enemy shall distress thee in all thy gates.

If thou wilt not observe to do all the words of this law that are written in this book, that thou mayest fear this glorious and fearful name, THE LORD YOUR GOD;

Then the Lord will make thy plagues wonderful, and the plagues of thy see, even great plagues, and of long continuance, and sore sickness, and of long continuance.

Moreover he will bring upon thee all the diseases of Egypt, which thou wast afraid of; and they shall cleave unto thee.

Also every sickness and every plague, which is not written in the book of this law, them will the Lord bring upon thee, until thou be destroyed.

And ye shall be left few in number, whereas ye were as the stars of heaven for multitude; because thou wouldest not obey the voice of the Lord thy God.

And it shall come to pass, that as the Lord rejoiced over you to do you good and multiply you; so the Lord will rejoice over you to destroy you, and to bring you to nought; and ye shall be plucked from off the land whither thou goest to possess it.

And the Lord shall scatter thee among all people, from the one end of the earth even unto the other; and there thou shalt serve other gods, which neither thou nor thy fathers have known, even wood and stone.

And among these nations shalt thou find no ease, neither shall the sole of thy foot have rest: but the Lord shall give thee there a trembling heart, and failing of eyes, and sorrow of mind:

And thy life shall hang in doubt before thee; and thou shalt fear day and night, and shalt have none assurance of thy life:

In the morning thou shalt say, Would God it were even! and at even thou shalt say, Would God it were morning! for the fear of thine heart wherewith thou shalt fear, and for the sight of thine eyes which thou shalt see.

And the Lord shall bring thee into Egypt again with ships, by the way whereof I spake unto thee, Thou shalt see it no more again: and there ye shall be sold unto your enemies for bondmen and bondwomen, and no man shall buy you.

And all these curses will remain upon the people until they obey the voice of the Lord God and do all that he commanded them to do. The people with all of their heart and with all of their soul must return to God, adults and children, and the Lord God will bring them back from captivity and have compassion upon them and restore them.

Thus ends the reading Answering America's Problem, amen.

www.ingramcontent.com/pod-product-compliance
Lightning Source LLC
Chambersburg PA
CBHW031238280526
45784CB00004B/1620